# The Broken Heart

## THE NEW MERMAIDS

General editor: Brian Gibbons
Professor of English Literature, University of Münster

Previous general editors have been
Philip Brockbank
Brian Morris
Roma Gill

# THE NEW MERMAIDS

The Alchemist
All for Love
Arden of Faversham
The Atheist's Tragedy
Bartholmew Fair
The Beaux' Stratagem
The Broken Heart
Bussy D'Ambois
The Changeling
A Chaste Maid in Cheapside
The Country Wife
The Critic
The Devil's Law-Case
The Double-Dealer
Dr Faustus
The Duchess of Malfi
Eastward Ho!
Edward the Second
Epicoene *or* The Silent Woman
Every Man in His Humour
A Fair Quarrel
An Ideal Husband
The Importance of Being Earnest
The Jew of Malta
The Knight of the Burning Pestle
Lady Windermere's Fan
London Assurance
Love for Love
The Malcontent
The Man of Mode
Marriage A-la-Mode
A New Way to Pay Old Debts
The Plain Dealer
The Playboy of the Western World
The Provoked Wife
The Recruiting Officer
The Relapse
The Revenger's Tragedy
The Rivals
The School for Scandal
She Stoops to Conquer
The Shoemaker's Holiday
The Spanish Tragedy
Tamburlaine
Three Late Medieval Morality Plays
  Mankind
  Everyman
  Mundus et Infans
Thyestes
'Tis Pity She's a Whore
Volpone
The Way of the World
The White Devil
The Witch
A Woman Killed with Kindness
A Woman of No Importance
Women Beware Women

# The Broken Heart

JOHN FORD

*Edited by*

BRIAN MORRIS

*Formerly Principal,*
*St David's University College,*
*Lampeter*

LONDON / A & C BLACK

NEW YORK / W W NORTON

*Reissued 1994*
*A & C Black (Publishers) Limited*
*35 Bedford Row, London WC1R 4JH*
*ISBN 0–7136–4098–7*

*First published in this form 1965*
*by Ernest Benn Limited*



*Published in the United States of America by*
*W. W. Norton and Company Inc.*
*500 Fifth Avenue, New York, N.Y. 10110*
*ISBN 0–393–90075–4*

*A CIP catalogue record for this book*
*is available from the British Library*
*and the Library of Congress.*

*Printed in Great Britain by*
*Biddles Ltd, Guildford and King's Lynn*

# CONTENTS

## ACKNOWLEDGEMENTS

*The Works of John Ford*, edited by Gifford and revised by Dyce (1869) is still the standard edition, and all editors of Ford are in its debt. I have also made use of Havelock Ellis's original *Mermaid* edition (1888), Smeaton's edition of *The Broken Heart* (1906), Sherman's edition of *'Tis Pity She's a Whore* and *The Broken Heart*, Boston and London, n.d., De Vocht's reprint, Louvain, 1927, and the editions in *Elizabethan and Stuart Plays*, ed. Baskervill, Heltzel and Nethercot, New York, 1934, *English Drama 1580–1642*, ed. Brooke and Paradise, Boston, 1933, and *The Anchor Anthology of Jacobean Drama*, ed. Richard C. Harrier, New York, 1963. My sincere thanks are also due to my colleagues at the University of Reading, and to the General Editor.

# INTRODUCTION

## THE AUTHOR

Deep In a dumpe Iacke forde alone was gott
W$^{th}$ folded Armes and Melancholye hatt,
(William Hemminge, *Elegy on Randolph's Finger*)

John Ford was baptized at Ilsington, Devonshire, on April 17th, 1586. Nothing is known of his early years, or his education, but he was admitted to the Middle Temple on November 16th, 1602. Several of his relations were already members, and others followed him there. In the Hilary Term of 1605/6 he was expelled for failing to pay his buttery bill (a common offence) and was not re-admitted until June 10th, 1608. He was certainly resident thereafter until 1617, and probably practised law in some capacity, though the records show that he was never called to the bar. From 1606 on he published several small works in prose and verse, but there is no certain evidence that he wrote anything for the stage before 1621. Between 1621 and 1625 he collaborated with Thomas Dekker and others in at least five plays, including *The Witch of Edmonton* and the masque, *The Sun's Darling*. After 1625 Ford probably worked alone. He contributed commendatory verses to plays by Webster, Shirley, Massinger, Brome and others, and a poem to the memorial volume for Ben Jonson, *Jonsonus Virbius*. His three greatest plays, *'Tis Pity She's a Whore*, *The Broken Heart*, and *Perkin Warbeck*, belong to the period 1625–34, when Ford was writing first for the King's Company and then for Christopher Beeston's companies at the Phoenix. The last of his plays known to have been produced in his lifetime is *The Lady's Trial* (early summer 1638) and nothing is known of Ford's life after that date. It was published early in 1639 with prefatory matter by the dramatist, and it is generally assumed that he died soon after.

See M. J. Sargeaunt, *John Ford*, Oxford, 1935, 1–31, and G. E. Bentley, *The Jacobean and Caroline Stage*, Oxford, 1956, iii, 433 ff.

## DATE AND SOURCES

*The Broken Heart* was entered on the Stationers' Register on 28th March, 1633, and published by Hugh Beeston in the same year. The title-page states that the play had been 'Acted By the King's Majesties Seruants at the priuate House in the Black-friers', and contains Ford's anagram 'Fide Honor' though not his name. The precise date of composition is unknown. W. J. Lawrence (*T.L.S.*, 12th July, 1923) argues for 1631–33 on the evidence of the reference to the miscellany 'The Garland of Good-will' at IV.ii, 15. This miscellany had been published in 1631, but it is now known that it had appeared in the Stationers' Register as early as 1593, and there is some evidence of an edition in 1604 (see F. O. Mann, *The Works of Thomas Deloney*, pp. xii and 562–3). Nevertheless, the 1631 edition might well have aroused interest, and its evidence should not be completely discounted. Bentley suggests a wider date-bracket:

> Twelve of Ford's seventeen known plays can be assigned to acting companies on the basis of external evidence. Eliminating the collaborations with Dekker, we find that three plays were performed by the King's company and five by Beeston's companies at the Phoenix. None of the plays for Beeston can be shown to be before 1630, but of the three for the King's company *The Lover's Melancholy* was licensed by Herbert 24 November 1628, *Beauty in a Trance* was acted at court 28 November 1630, and the third is *The Broken Heart*. . . . *The Broken Heart* must have been close in date to *Beauty in a Trance* and *The Lover's Melancholy*, or about 1627–31.[1]

This is probably as accurate as it is possible to be, though the available evidence is so meagre as to make any dating no more than conjectural.

No single source has been discovered for the plot, and it is probable that none exists. One couplet in the prologue has aroused comment:

> What may be here thought a fiction, when time's youth
> Wanted some riper years, was known a truth:

S. P. Sherman argued[2] that Ford intended the play to echo

[1] Bentley, *op. cit.*, iii. 441–2.
[2] S. P. Sherman, 'Stella and *The Broken Heart*', *PMLA*, XXIV, 1909, 274–285.

the relationship between Sir Philip Sidney and Penelope Rich, and although the love-story and the play end very differently this may well be true. Giovanni M. Carsaniga adds another incident.[1] On March 17th, 1551, in Antwerp, the Lucchese merchant Simone Turchi killed his fellow citizen Jeronimo Deodati by using exactly the same kind of chair as Orgilus uses to kill Ithocles in Ford's play. The fact was widely recorded, and the best description is given in Matteo Bandello's *Novelle* (Part Four) entitled 'Simone Turchi ha nemistà con Gieronimo Deodati lucchese . . .' This was first mentioned as a possible source for the play by Dyce, but he seems not to have realized that it was an account of an historical event, and therefore relevant to the couplet in the prologue. Speaking of that couplet Carsaniga concludes, 'He does not mean that his entire plot closely follows a single story, but that some of the events in his tragedy (at least two, we contend) had their origin in some real happenings'. Finally, although the general indebtedness of Ford's play to Sidney's *Arcadia* has been noticed, I would draw attention to the particular story of Argalus and Parthenia,[2] which shares several details with the story of Orgilus and Penthea and celebrates the same qualities of heroic calm in a tragic situation.

[1] G. M. Carsaniga, ' "The Truth" in John Ford's *The Broken Heart*', *Comparative Literature*, X, 1958, 344–8.
[2] Sidney, *Arcadia*, ed. Feuillerat, I, 5–8.

## THE PLAY

Eliot, when he selected the lines

> Remember,
> When we last gathered roses in the garden,
> I found my wits; but truly you lost yours.

as 'perhaps the purest poetry to be found in the whole of Ford's writings'[1] was saluting the achievement of a tone which he himself has supremely commanded in our age. The stillness, the untroubled rhythms, the verbal control which at once mask and mediate the instant of passion are properties shared by both poets. In other respects they are different; only in this transpicuous simplicity of tone do their worlds, for a moment, touch. Yet it is perhaps this very affinity which vitiates Eliot's insight into the rest of Ford's dramatic work. *Perkin Warbeck* is, for him, 'unquestionably Ford's highest achievement', and he severely qualifies his praise of *The Broken Heart*:

> the plot is somewhat overloaded and distracted by the affairs of unfortunate personages, all of whom have an equal claim on our attention;

Few have agreed with Eliot's evaluation, but his remarks do draw attention to the fact that *The Broken Heart* is a play without a protagonist, built up of several plots, and populated with 'unfortunate' people. The multiplicity is organized to subserve an exploration of certain abnormal states of mind, certain peripheral situations, which meet, clash, and break upon one another. Ford's purpose in this play is to contemplate and anatomize humanity in some of its most egregious conditions.

### THEMES

Una Ellis-Fermor, summing up the play, refers to its celebration of 'the immutable virtues; courage, continence, and chivalry',[2] and her phrase marks off the narrow areas

[1] T. S. Eliot, 'John Ford' in *Selected Essays*, and reprinted in *Elizabethan Dramatists*, p. 126.
[2] *The Jacobean Drama*, p. 246.

of experience within which Ford works. Courage is the central virtue in his presentation of the theme of Endurance. Evil is a minimal presence in the play; the great adversary of the human spirit is suffering, and it is in the presence of suffering that courage is established—courage which is self-affirmation in the face of situations which threaten personal integrity. The play opens with an act of renunciation by Orgilus. He undertakes his 'voluntary exile'

> First, by my absence to take off the cares
> Of jealous Bassanes; but chiefly, sir,
> To free Penthea from a hell on earth;
> Lastly, to lose the memory of something
> Her presence makes to live in me afresh.

His motives are at once unselfish and self-affirming, for the 'memory' is potentially destructive in his present circumstances. On this occasion his courage is short-lived; he returns in disguise (I.iii) to watch over the progress of events. The theme is taken up, centrally, by Penthea, who begins, like so many of Ford's heroes and heroines, by electing to play a role which is contrary to her true nature. She first appears (II.i) as the resigned, dutiful, contained wife of a morbidly jealous husband. Everything is subdued to achieving the role imposed upon her by her marriage to Bassanes:

> I need
> No braveries nor cost of art, to draw
> The whiteness of my name into offence . . .

This offer of endurance is attacked by Orgilus in II.iii as unnatural, inhuman, but she rejects him; his love is a threat to the integrity she has assumed. The iron core of principle is stated by Prophilus at the end of Act II:

> He cannot fear
> Who builds on noble grounds; sickness or pain
> Is the deserver's exercise . . .

In the long dialogue with her brother Ithocles in III.ii the tension between desire and duty is increased, and Penthea's agony finds refuge in paradox. She sees herself, in honouring her marriage, as 'a spotted whore',

> For she that's wife to Orgilus, and lives
> In known adultery with Bassanes,
> Is at the best a whore.

This self-knowledge (or self-delusion) is the crucial point in Ford's exploration of Endurance through the figure of Penthea. Once she has established the paradox, her logic is remorseless. Whores must be punished, and since no one else believes her to be a whore she must punish herself. She goes about it protractedly, arranging her affairs in the 'will-scene' with Calantha (III.v), enduring the decay of her reason, and finally starving herself to death. Her renunciation reaps no reward, but she is surrounded in Acts IV and V with examples of creative suffering, or, at least, suffering which does not cripple before it destroys. Her husband Bassanes, who, in the earlier acts, endures torments of jealousy, undertakes his own cure, and emerges in IV.ii armed with a stoic fortitude against the assaults of passion.[1] It is immediately tested by confrontation with Orgilus and then with the mad Penthea, and his reaction is to endure, open-eyed and unflinching, the expiatory agony. This suffering is therapeutic, and he stands at the end of the play fit to be 'Sparta's marshal'. His courage allows him to affirm his true nature. Similarly, Ithocles, when confronted with Penthea's madness, takes his stand upon an endurance which is the refusal of sensation:

On my soul
Lies such an infinite clog of massy dullness,
As that I have not sense enough to feel it.

This withdrawal becomes a self-affirmative courage at the moment he faces death:

Strike home. A courage
As keen as thy revenge shall give it welcome.

Courageous endurance is the dominant quality in Calantha's attitude to news in the dance scene (V.ii), where she refuses to allow accumulated disasters to disrupt 'the custom of this ceremony'. Orgilus, in the self-chosen manner of his death, endures the literal withdrawal of sensation, and his previous sufferings are subsumed in the slow expiation. He invites the onlookers to 'look upon my steadiness', and as the standard falls 'Of my prerogative in being a creature' Bassanes isolates the quality of his endurance in the phrase 'this pastime Appears majestical'. Ford presents Endurance as both creative and tragic. It is the dynamic of Penthea's

[1] Ford's debt to Burton's *Anatomy of Melancholy* in the character of Bassanes, and elsewhere, is fully discussed in S. B. Ewing's *Burtonian Melancholy in the Plays of John Ford*, Princeton, 1940.

deluded self-sacrifice, as well as of Bassanes' resolute self-cure. The 'deserver's exercise' can be transmuted by the deserver's courage.

Courage is linked with Continence as self-affirmation through Endurance is with self-restraint. Ford exhibits this restraint in two forms: as continence of action and continence of feeling. In human action, the two great hazards are seen as Ambition and Rashness. In I.i Orgilus, rehearsing the recent history of Sparta, explains how the death of Thrasus had prevented the ambitions for happiness which he shared with Penthea. Her brother Ithocles 'proud of youth, and prouder in his power' had brought about the present disastrous situation by the forced marriage of his sister to Bassanes 'a nobleman, in honour And riches, I confess, beyond my fortunes'. Ithocles himself, in soliloquy (II.ii), condemns Ambition (' 'tis of vipers' breed: it gnaws A passage through the womb that gave it motion'), and states the moral norm of the play:

Morality, applied
To timely practice, keeps the soul in tune,
At whose sweet music all our actions dance.

Tecnicus, the play's commentator, pays homage to the same mean in his advice to Orgilus:

Neglects in young men of delights, and life,
Run often to extremities; they care not
For harms to others, who contemn their own.

He continues to warn throughout the play ('let not a resolution Of giddy rashness choke the breath of reason' III.i, 1) and his prophecy 'Revenge proves its own executioner' is recalled by Orgilus at the moment of his death. The harmonious dance of actions, motivated by 'morality', is the ideal of behaviour in the play, and it is the disruption of this harmony by actions stemming from Ambition and Rashness which finally bring about the superb irony of Calantha's dance in the final Act.

Continence of feeling is much more delicately enunciated, and it remains an impression after the play rather than a present concern in its development. It seems the proper behaviour of these people to avoid the excesses both of grief and joy. Ithocles, returning home in triumph, crowned with a provincial garland (I.ii), displays the acceptable attitudes, controlling the joy with his humility, modestly distributing the honour upon his friends and soldiers. This restraint upon joy, narrowing, focusing the emotional range of the play, is carried through by the grave decorum of the court. Amyclas is constantly aware of what seems to him an undue seriousness in those around him ('Our court wears gravity more than we relish' III.iii, 39; 'But wherefore sits the court in such a silence?' IV.iii, 69), yet the dominant tone of this egregious society continues solemn, until it becomes tragic. There are two scenes, in particular, where Ford's characters sin against continence of feeling. In the first (III.ii), Bassanes, sick with jealousy, bursts in upon Penthea and Ithocles with the significant words 'I can forbear no longer'. He accuses them of pride, lechery, incest, in an outburst of peculiar savagery. The other characters immediately explain his behaviour as 'distraction', 'most admirable lunacy' or drunkenness, and Grausis speaks for them when she says: 'These are his megrims, firks, and melancholies'. The outburst is soon over, but Ithocles refuses to give him charge of his wife again until

> . . . you shall show good proof that manly wisdom,
> Not overswayed by passion, or opinion,
> Knows how to lead your judgement

In the second (IV.ii), Penthea's restraint breaks down and her feelings overflow. This is the freedom of emotion given by madness, and Ithocles' response is one of pity ('Poor soul, how idly Her fancies guide her tongue'). Yet even here she is vaguely conscious of the accepted standards:

> Goodness! we had been happy; too much happiness
> Will make folk proud, they say . . .

Continence of feeling issues in a rare delicacy of emotion and response (which is one of Ford's great achievements in drama). Penthea's mad-scene stands in strong contrast to her previous appearance (III.v) when she asks Calantha to be her executrix. This scene is a masterly organization of subtle states of feeling, beginning with courtly decorum, establishing slowly Penthea's sad, calm apprehensions of death, moving through the stately formality of the 'humble suit', to the tender revelation of her brother's love to the Princess:

> Look on him, princess, with an eye of pity;
> How like the ghost of what he late appeared
> 'A moves before you.

The reticence in this dialogue between two women is essentially a full awareness of each other's sensibilities, a tenderness to offend, so that communication develops through graded shifts and nuances of tone, through verbal restraints, and by the physical presence of one person before another. Ford's art is totally dramatic, and in this scene words are used as much to muffle and subdue emotions as to mediate them. In the following act Penthea goes mad and dies, but Calantha grows in dramatic stature until the play's supreme example of continence, the dance-scene. Here physical action is played against mental stasis, social interchange against personal isolation. Calantha both controls and is controlled, and the pattern of the dance, which symbolizes the body politic, dominates the succession of disasters through Calantha's continent, restraining will. Ford's exploration of Restraint encompasses both the most delicate responses of person to person, and the stern government of the passions, incident to those who rule.

Chivalry is the translation into 'timely practice' of the concept of Honour, which is the third of Ford's themes. Honour is not a major concern in the early scenes, though several of the characters discuss it (e.g. I.iii, 55–59). It first becomes a criterion of action in II.iii, when Penthea is decoyed into the garden, and faces Orgilus. Her first response is a defence of her compromised honour:

> Rash man. Thou layest
> A blemish on mine honour, with the hazard
> Of thy too desperate life . . .

For her, at this point, her honour—the honour of a faithful though unwilling wife—is the keystone of her personal integrity, and she defends it fiercely. The past is buried, and rather than recall it, she impugns the 'honour' of Orgilus:

> . . . I find
> The constant preservation of thy merit,
> By thy not daring to attempt my fame
> With injury of any loose conceit,
> Which might give deeper wounds to discontents.

Her conception of his 'honour' is as a quality which preserves the personalities of others inviolate, and is especially careful of her female 'virtue'. When this check is ineffective she openly threatens his good name in society:

> Your reputation (if you value any)
> Lies bleeding at my feet.

Orgilus reacts by rejecting words altogether ('Action, not words, shall show me') and Penthea, left alone for a moment, reverts to her first conception of honour as a principle of behaviour:

> Honour,
> How much we fight with weakness to preserve thee.

What emerges from this scene is that Penthea has a complex, if confused, idea of honour as an amalgam of female virtue, masculine forbearance, and social reputation. Orgilus has no corresponding code of chivalry, and in the following scene (III.i) he seems to envisage it as a form of integrity, a correspondence between seeming and being:

> Could art
> Run through mine inmost thoughts, it should not sift
> An inclination there more than what suited
> With justice of mine honour.

This simple view draws from Tecnicus a long exposition of the true nature of Honour, which is Ford's central statement of the theme in the play:

> But know then, Orgilus, what honour is:
> Honour consists not in a bare opinion
> By doing any act that feeds content,
> Brave in appearance, 'cause we think it brave;
> Such honour comes by accident, not nature,
> Proceeding from the vices of our passion,
> Which makes our reason drunk. But real honour
> Is the reward of virtue, and acquired
> By justice, or by valour which for basis
> Hath justice to uphold it. He then fails
> In honour, who for lucre or revenge
> Commits thefts, murthers, treasons, and adulteries,
> With such like, by intrenching on just laws,
> Whose sovereignty is best preserved by justice.
> Thus, as you see how honour must be grounded
> On knowledge, not opinion—for opinion
> Relies on probability and accident,
> But knowledge on necessity and truth—
> I leave thee to the fit consideration
> Of what becomes the grace of real honour . . .

Honour, for Tecnicus, and for the moral fabric of this play, is a virtue rooted in society, a reward given for knowledge exercised in the preservation of justice and truth. It is not an isolated, personal quality, still less an accidental valour, but a pattern of behaviour lived out in the presence of others. By this ideal the subsequent actions of the characters are to be judged, and our attention is focused primarily on the figures of Orgilus and Ithocles. Orgilus' relentless pursuit of revenge must stand condemned as dishonourable, yet it is a failure conditioned by events, and palliated by his unique chivalry towards his victim. Ithocles is killed with consummate courtesy, and the scene of his death is almost a contest of honourable attitudes Orgilus speaks of it as a 'sacrifice', and Ithocles retorts by refusing to 'whine and beg compassion'. He adopts a higher attitude:

> A statelier resolution arms my confidence,
> To cozen thee of honour . . .

He calls Orgilus 'a slave', and the revenge 'a murther'. Orgilus, in killing him, adjures him to

> Keep up thy spirit:
> I will be gentle even in blood; to linger
> Pain, which I strive to cure, were to be cruel.

By the terms of the play Ithocles makes an honourable end, with forgiveness in his last words and malice towards none. Orgilus recognizes both the ethical superiority of his victim's life, and his own deeply marred virtue, and his final couplet in this scene is richly ambivalent:

> In vain they build their hopes whose life is shame:
> No monument lasts but a happy name.

Honour, in Ford's presentation of it, is no mere scutcheon; it is a quality of life, an ideal lived out in public action and service, which moulds the inward man.

The setting in which these themes are developed is, most appropriately, Sparta. It is the Sparta not only of Sidney's *Arcadia*, but of Plutarch's *Life of Lycurgus* as well;[1] a state devoted to the cultivation of the masculine virtues of Endurance, Restraint, and Honour, existing on a sparse collocation of iron principles, anti-intellectual (Orgilus could not live in Athens, and Tecnicus deserts Sparta in the end), fearless, rigorous, and pure. These are the values which the play cherishes, and which the themes enunciate.

## Structure

Structure is the way art organizes experience, and

[1] Plutarch's account of Sparta and the Spartan virtues is discussed in F. Ollier's *Le Mirage Spartiate*, Paris, 1933, ii, 165–215.

dramatic structure has usually been thought of in terms of the 'kinds'—tragedy, comedy, history, pastoral and the like. The title-page of the 1633 Quarto of *The Broken Heart* declares it to be a Tragedy, the Prologue invites us to 'partake a pity with delight' yet in any formal sense the tragic pattern is blurred, dissipated, and finally fragmentary. As a 'de casibus' tragedy, about the fall of a noble man, it reads queerly; the major characters are neither great nor little, there is no fall from great happiness to deep despair, because no great happiness has ever existed in the play. Despite this, allegiances to the tragic pattern are strong, and the dominant feature is a sense of 'Ate', an infatuation or moral blindness, in which right and wrong, advantage and disadvantage are indistinguishable. Orgilus is obsessed with Revenge, despite all Tecnicus can say to him; Penthea with self-destruction as the punishment for her sins; Ithocles with personal honour, disregarding the anger of Orgilus; and Calantha with ritual self-immolation, in spite of her country's need. As Kaufmann says:[1]

> The strange silences which attend the movements of Ford's heroes have been remarked by critics. They are silent because their personal reasons are sufficient; the world's claims are thus not opposed and equal, but negligible and incommensurate.

It is a world of immovable commitments which the characters have contracted for themselves, and the contracts issue in suffering and death. Experientially, the tragic effects of pity and fear are powerfully present, but the formal aspect of tragedy (like so many other things in the play) is muted and restrained.

Similarly, it is insufficient to think of the play in terms of the Revenge ethic, although revenge is the strongest motivating force in the play's action. It is a latent presence, delayed, protracted, until IV.ii, when Orgilus, reminded of his self-imposed duty by the allusions in Penthea's mad words, says,

> She has tutored me;
> Some powerful inspiration checks my laziness . . .

Thereafter it is prepared in private and executed in public, and the privacy of Orgilus' thought is, to say the least, unconventional. I know no other Jacobean play in which the

[1] R. J. Kaufmann, 'Ford's Tragic Perspective', in *Elizabethan Drama: Modern Essays in Criticism*, ed. Kaufmann, New York and Oxford, p. 362.

figure of the revenger is presented with this degree of self-sufficiency. The audience is never permitted to share Orgilus' reasons; his thoughts are always his own. The action of revenge is taken wide-eyed and in cold blood. Ithocles is caught in the chair, and Orgilus reviles the 'insulting Phaeton' with ironies that are as much defensive as vengeful:

> . . . Penthea's groans and tortures,
> Her agonies, her miseries, afflictions,
> Ne'er touched upon your thought. As for my injuries,
> Alas, they were beneath your royal pity;
> But yet they lived, thou proud man, to confound thee.

Even in recounting the murder (V.ii) Orgilus is aptly laconic; his conciseness reflects his own complete satisfaction with the justice of the act:

> . . . This weapon
> Was instrument to my revenge. The reasons
> Are just, and known; quit him of these, and then
> Never lived gentleman of greater merit,
> Hope, or abiliment to steer a kingdom.

Yet to label *The Broken Heart* as a revenge tragedy is to elect Orgilus as the protagonist, to subdue the greater part of the drama, and to falsify Ford's careful distribution of emphases. Revenge alone is not a sufficiently powerful dynamic.

The central structural feature, as Blayney has pointed out,[1] is the problem of the enforced marriage and its consequences. Before the play begins Orgilus and Penthea had gone through a formal betrothal, or pre-contract of marriage. In seventeenth century England this required only the verbally expressed agreement to marry of the two parties, usually (but not necessarily) in the presence of witnesses. This ceremony was binding, and rendered invalid the subsequent marriage to another of either man or woman. Thus, the vows made by Penthea and Orgilus, presumably in the presence of their fathers, were far stronger than simple affirmations of love. They were vows of betrothal, and her subsequent enforced marriage to Bassanes would have been thought adulterous.[2] The theme was neither unconventional

[1] Glenn H. Blayney, 'Convention, Plot, and Structure in *The Broken Heart*', *Modern Philology*, LVI, 1958, pp. 1–9. What follows is much indebted to this article.

[2] This is the view Penthea takes (III.ii, 68–78) and Orgilus endorses.

nor novel when Ford took it up. The problems of the pre-contract and the betrothal had exercised Shakespeare, in *Measure for Measure*,[1] the marriage theme is the subject of George Wilkins' *The Miseries of Enforced Marriage*, and many other plays between 1600 and 1630 deal with these topics. Penthea's description of herself as one who lives in adultery with Bassanes is quite in accord with seventeenth century views; what is peculiarly Ford's is the course she takes to deal with the situation. The supremely evil act, in *The Broken Heart*, is the enforcement of her marriage with Bassanes, and it is from this that the tragic events ensue. Structurally, the play is best seen as a study of the contemporary problem of the pre-contract and the enforced marriage.

There are three pairs of lovers in the play—Penthea and Orgilus, Ithocles and Calantha, and Prophilus and Euphranea. The last pair act as a norm, and a foil to the other two. In the first scene of the play Orgilus makes his sister Euphranea promise that she will not pledge herself to any man without his, as well as her father's, consent. The reason for this is stated clearly:

> It shall be my first care to see thee matched
> As may become thy choice and our contents.

He has already shown how Ithocles, Penthea's brother, has ignored the free choice of his sister, and the suffering that this has brought. His view of marriage is that it should be based on free choice and family concurrence. Both sides hold to the agreement; Euphranea (as Orgilus sees) insists on obtaining her brother's consent before she accepts Prophilus' offer of marriage, and Orgilus, despite the close friendship of Prophilus and Ithocles, agrees to the match ('My sister's marriage With Prophilus is from my heart confirmed'). This marriage is happy, and it stands in strong contrast to the progress of the other pairs of lovers. These four characters develop through scenes of parting or coming together. The first of these (II.iii) is a scene of rejection. Penthea has retreated to the iron principle that her marriage to Bassanes represents her integrity as a person. Orgilus remains equally firm upon what is now an unrealistic principle:

> Penthea is the wife to Orgilus,
> And ever shall be.

[1] See Ernest Schanzer, *The Problem Plays of Shakespeare*, 1963, pp. 75–9.

Penthea's reply 'Never shall nor will' represents the stalemate, and they part. This movement asunder is balanced in III.ii by the coming together of Ithocles and Penthea. The insistence here is upon kinship and family ties ('We had one father, in one womb took life'), and Ithocles' deep grief and repentance for the suffering he has caused his sister creates a harmony between them which is deepened by the disclosure of his own love for Calantha. This harmony survives the frantic intrusion of Bassanes, and the scene ends with Ithocles taking his sister into his own care. The fifth scene of Act III presents the delicate encounter between Calantha and Penthea. This is superficially a scene of parting, since Penthea is appointing an executrix to attend to her affairs after her death, but the deeper movement of the dialogue is an attempt to initiate a social intimacy which will allow Penthea to commend her brother to Calantha's love. As a formal gesture this meets with rejection ('Your check lies in my silence'), but the shared confidences, the matched proprieties, unite the two women in an understanding which belies the surface statement. The following scene (IV.i),[1] in which Ithocles is insulted by Nearchus, and befriended by Orgilus, is an ironic comment on the achieved intimacy of the two women. Orgilus, in offering friendship, makes a series of comments which are richly ambiguous:

In point of honour
Discretion knows no bounds. Amelus told me
'Twas all about a little ring . . .

A lady's favour
Is not to be so slighted . . .

Griefs will have their vent.

The friendship is bait for the trap. In IV.ii, Penthea's mad-scene, she has, in effect, retreated from contact with other people, and inhabits a calm, dream-world of her own. Yet her parting from the other characters is not complete; her errant phrases establish the vital link with her lover and spur him to the accomplishment of revenge. This tenuous link is all that is left of the once vital intimacy of Penthea and Orgilus, the frustration of which at the beginning of the play is the cause of all the action. As Penthea and Orgilus are forced apart, so Ithocles and Calantha come together, and in IV.iii there is what the contemporary

[1] From this point the tempo of the lovers' progress increases; the pattern develops unhindered in successive scenes.

audience would have accepted as a formal betrothal. The King joins their hands, and says 'Calantha, take thine own'; Calantha accepts Ithocles—'Thou'rt mine'—and later Ithocles tells Orgilus 'The princess is contracted mine'. With the reiterated friendship between Orgilus and Ithocles in this scene the series of misalliances is complete; Orgilus and Penthea have been driven apart, Ithocles and Calantha have come together, Ithocles and Orgilus appear friends, Penthea and Calantha have established a rich, if delicate, relationship. From Orgilus' point of view the time is ripe for one violent action which will right all injustices. This complex pattern of uniting and parting is brought about by the enforced marriage from which the play begins, and the key to the structure of the play is the ritual working out of the misalliance. All attempts at redemption are futile.

This thematic pattern is complemented by another, theatrical, structure. In the theatre the prevailing impression is of a play in which deep stillness often makes the dramatic point. There is very little action, characters come and go, usually in ceremonial groups and processions, and dialogues frequently reach the very edge of silence before the pressure is released. Visual impressions in the first four acts are slight—a court, a garden, a bedchamber—and several of the scenes are simply semi-localized encounters between people. Through this austere dramaturgy the plot builds up to the three great, 'spectacular' scenes at the end of the play: the death of Ithocles, the dance scene, and the final scene in the temple. Ford's stage-directions are unusually detailed, and they give precise indications for the playing of these scenes. The importance of spectacle in Ford's plays has been generally agreed, but seldom investigated in any detail. The vital point is that they are exercises in deepened dramatic perspective. At the death of Ithocles the spectacle is created through the dramatic action. When Ithocles and Orgilus enter (IV.iv) the stage presents no more than a ritual scene of mourning; three chairs, one of them containing the dead, veiled body of Penthea, and two maids sitting at her feet. The audience, alerted by the servant's words (''Tis done; that on her right hand'), is aware of some impending but unspecified treachery, yet the opening dialogue is conventional lamentation mediating the facts in an unimpassioned way. When Ithocles sits down, is caught in the chair, and murdered, the spectacle is created. Orgilus has placed side by side the murdered man and his self-slaughtered sister; he has made the visual equation between Penthea, trapped in her marriage situation, and Ithocles locked in the chair; his blood for her forced faith. And he is aware of this as a spectacle. The last words of the scene emphasize the emblematic quality of the stage-picture:

> Sweet twins, shine stars for ever.
> In vain they build their hopes whose life is shame:
> No monument lasts but a happy name.

The scene which contains the dance, and the death of Orgilus (V.ii) is a heightened example of the same dramatic technique. Once again, the stage directions are specific; there is loud music, a processional entry, and 'all make a stand'. A conscious decorum is enacted in the ritual of the dance, and the fact that no messengers of death are allowed to disrupt the pattern establishes the 'masculine spirit' and the dramatic primacy of Calantha. Not only is this scene a spectacle to an audience, it becomes a spectacle to those on stage as well. As one report of death follows another, and still the dance goes on, Armostes, Bassanes, and Orgilus are made aware of the symbolic quality of the situation: endurance, fortitude, continence of feeling, proper honour, are being played out on this stage-upon-a-stage, not in words but in articulate action. The death of Orgilus, which ends this scene, is a spectacle of a complementary kind. Here too the characters are conscious that they are acting parts in a public performance. Bassanes says:

> This pastime
> Appears majestical; some high-tuned poem
> Hereafter shall deliver to posterity
> The writer's glory and his subject's triumph.

In the slow, ritual death by bleeding the correspondences are again created in visual terms rather than in words. As Penthea has died by her own hand, so does Orgilus; as the courtly proprieties have been observed in the dance, so they are here ('How is't man? Droop not yet.'); as Ithocles bled for Penthea, so Orgilus bleeds for Ithocles. These scenes are at once public and intensely personal, a duality epitomized in the last scene of the play, which takes place in the temple. The altar is white, the women are dressed in white, symbol of purity and death, and all the characters, living and dead, are assembled with the exceptions of Orgilus and Penthea. The scene begins with worship, which is both public and private, and this creates the double perspective, since the audience is watching a spectacle and the characters are consciously enacting one. Worship gives place to statecraft, the proper ordering of the country's affairs and the just bestowal of rewards and settlements, and when this is complete, Calantha performs the final symbolic act:

> Thus I new-marry him whose wife I am;

The living Calantha and the dead Ithocles complete the regression of the spectacle, for her action is performed both within the image which the court is consciously creating in its ritual, and before the audience. In this fulfilment of her pre-contract she is ironically recalling the pre-contract of Orgilus and Penthea, and this complex perspective accomplishes the prophecy of Tecnicus:

> The lifeless trunk shall wed the broken heart.

It takes place in a moment of intense stillness. As Calantha says, echoing Seneca,

> They are the silent griefs which cut the heart-strings.

### Language

Eliot ends his essay on Ford with these words:

> The varieties of cadence and tone in blank verse are none too many, in the history of English verse; and Ford, though intermittently, was able to manipulate sequences of words in blank verse in a manner which is quite his own.

The most memorable passages in Ford's plays are those in which he matches a grave simplicity of rhythm and phrase with an aristocratic refinement of theme. The best exemplar is probably Eroclea's speech in *The Lover's Melancholy*, IV.iii:

> Minutes are numbered by the fall of sands,
> As by an hourglass; the span of time
> Doth waste us to our graves, and we look on it:
> An age of pleasure, revelled out, comes home
> At last, and ends in sorrow; but the life,
> Weary of riot, numbers every sand,
> Wailing in sighs, until the last drop down;
> So to conclude calamity in rest.

It is this attenuated, gaunt dignity of tone which all Ford's critics have praised, but his peculiar dialect has a wider range, his verbal landscape is more subtly graded.

Anderson, in his article on Ford's imagery,[1] establishes the close links between the 'heart' and 'banquet' images in *The Broken Heart* and *'Tis Pity She's a Whore* and speaks of Ford's masterful handling of imagery. But the immediate impression, in reading a play of Ford's, is that the language is remarkable for its lack of figures; its metaphors are seldom assertive. There is none of the virtuosity with language that is characteristic of so much of the writing of the Jacobean period. The true distinction is not between image and plain statement, but between periphrastic and direct utterance.

Ford's moments of profound simplicity are set in the context of an elaborate and courtly language, by means of which his speakers communicate both information and attitudes. Prophilus, describing Ithocles' return from the war, says to Calantha:

> Excellent princess,
> Your own fair eyes may soon report a truth
> Unto your judgement, with what moderation,
> Calmness of nature, measure, bounds, and limits
> Of thankfulness and joy, 'a doth digest
> Such amplitude of his success as would
> In others, moulded of a spirit less clear,
> Advance 'em to comparison with heaven.

Here the core of meaning is overlaid with a complicated yet loosely articulated syntax which gives, without recourse to verbal ingenuity, an aureate grandeur of utterance. And this is not deployed to delineate character: it is a feature common to most of the speakers in certain situations. Orgilus, later in the same act, says to Tecnicus:

> But I, most learned artist, am not so much
> At odds with nature that I grutch the thrift
> Of any true deserver; nor doth malice
> Of present hopes so check them with despair
> As that I yield to thought of more affliction
> Than what is incident to frailty . . .

This periphrastic manner imparts a social code, a civilized, ornate good manners in which statements are highly wrought before they are spoken, as a mark of respect. When this chivalrous awareness of others is lacking, as in

[1] Donald K. Anderson, Jr., 'The Heart and the Banquet: Imagery in Ford's '*'Tis Pity She's a Whore* and *The Broken Heart*', *Studies in English Literature* 1500–1900, II, 209–17.

the scenes where Bassanes' jealousy is rampant, the language takes on a brutal directness. Bassanes commands a wide range, from Jonsonian comic vigour—

> I'll have that window next the street dammed up;
> It gives too full a prospect to temptation,
> And courts a gazer's glances . . .

to a savagery which only Marston could match:

> Yes, and 'a knows
> To whom 'a talks; to one that franks his lust
> In swine-security of bestial incest.

Bassanes' language in the early acts is the closest contact the play makes with colloquial speech,[1] and it forms a series of violent contrasts with the prevailing mode. For the most part, the language is ceremoniously distanced from the normal speech of men, and after his reformation Bassanes learns to speak the true courtly tongue:

> How it was done let him report, the forfeit
> Of whose allegiance to our laws doth covet
> Rigour of justice; but that done it is,
> Mine eyes have been an evidence of credit
> Too sure to be convinced.

The periphrastic style is not single and inflexible. It functions to create a mannered atmosphere, but it is also present and active at moments of emotional complexity or rarity. For example, in I.iii. Orgilus apostrophizes Love:

> Love, thou art full of mystery! The deities
> Themselves are not secure in searching out
> The secrets of those flames, which, hidden, waste
> A breast made tributary to the laws
> Of beauty. Physic yet hath never found
> A remedy to cure a lover's wound.

The loosening of the syntax, and the consequent slight dislocation of the sense, evokes the feeling that the passage is made up of certain key words—'mystery' 'secure' 'secrets' 'flames' 'hidden' 'waste'—each energizing a phrase, and creating not a lucid statement but an arcane meditation. There is a dazzle on the surface of the words which blurs the edges of their meaning, and mediates a process of thought rather than the thought itself. This is even more apparent in Penthea's speech to Calantha in III.v, where

[1] Except the scene between the courtiers and the maids of honour (I.ii), which seems to me an unfortunate lapse on Ford's part.

she is talking about the inability of the world to minister to a troubled mind:

> Glories
> Of human greatness are but pleasing dreams,
> And shadows soon decaying; on the stage
> Of my mortality my youth hath acted
> Some scenes of vanity, drawn out at length
> By varied pleasures, sweetened in the mixture,
> But tragical in issue. Beauty, pomp,
> With every sensuality our giddiness
> Doth frame an idol, are unconstant friends,
> When any troubled passion makes assault
> On the unguarded castle of the mind.

This is a dream sequence, where impressions drift up from individual words and collect into a rarified mood. The periphrastic syntax is little more than a stream of half-consciousness, whose movement acts as an anodyne upon understanding.

In contrast, Ford's poetry of direct statement permits thought to function sensitively. At times, the method is to set off a vibrant line by placing it in a context of utter simplicity:

> We may stand up. Have you aught else to urge
> Of new demand? As for the old, forget it;
> 'Tis buried in an everlasting silence,
> And shall be, shall be ever. What more would ye?

More commonly, Ford's directness has a literary sanction. His debt to Webster in *The Broken Heart* is easily traced, and nowhere more evident than at those moments when his characters face death. The clearest example is provided by Orgilus in V.ii:

> *Bassanes*. Life's fountain is dried up.
> *Orgilus*. So falls the standard
> Of my prerogative in being a creature.
> A mist hangs o'er mine eyes, the sun's bright splendour
> Is clouded in an everlasting shadow.
> Welcome, thou ice, that sittest about my heart;
> No heat can ever thaw thee.
> *Nearchus*. Speech hath left him.
> *Bassanes*. 'A has shook hands with time.

These lines owe everything to the fifth act of *The White Devil*. Similarly, as Eliot has pointed out, Shakespeare stands behind Penthea's speech in the mad-scene, IV.ii:

Sure, if we were all Sirens, we should sing pitifully;
And 'twere a comely music, when in parts
One sung another's knell. The turtle sighs
When he hath lost his mate; and yet some say
'A must be dead first . . .

The moments when Ford's unique voice makes itself heard in simplicity have often been quoted. They frequently occur when the dramatic tension is high, and the most famous example is the last speech of Calantha, at V.iii, 62–76, where the symbolic action is frozen into immobility by the cold dignity and restraint of the words. But they also occupy less exalted situations. Ithocles, in IV.i, speaks of the happiness which does not depend upon illusion:

Yet these are still but dreams. Give me felicity
Of which my senses waking are partakers,
A real, visible, material happiness;
And then, too, when I stagger in expectance
Of the least comfort that can cherish life—
I saw it, sir, I saw it; for it came
From her own hand.

And Orgilus, after hearing the song which precedes Penthea's death, says, simply,

A horrid stillness
Succeeds this deathful air; let's know the reason.
Tread softly; there is mystery in mourning.

## THE TEXT

THERE is only one edition of this play, the Quarto of 1633. This is a badly printed text, with many literal errors, some speeches wrongly assigned (e.g. III.v, 36, IV.ii, 112), and several passages which are nonsense as they stand (e.g. II.iii, 30–3, III.ii, 54–8, III.ii, 205–6). All emendations are recorded in the Notes. This text has been prepared from Xerox prints of the British Museum copy, pressmark 644.b.35, which contains the uncorrected state of the inner forme of sheet B (see note to I.i, 31). It was collated against the Bodleian copy, Malone 205, and no substantive variants were found. Spelling and capitalization have been modernized throughout, and all Latin words in stage directions and Act and Scene headings have been translated, except 'Exeunt' and 'Manent'. Ford's stage directions are careful and detailed, and they are one of the reasons for believing that the copy for Q was the author's manuscript. The few editorial additions to the stage directions are enclosed in square brackets. Unemphatic forms of pronouns have been left as they stand in Q. The punctuation of Q is not regular, and does not form a good guide to the delivery of the verse. I have therefore modernized it whenever I felt it necessary to do so, in the interests of syntactical intelligibility.

## DISTRIBUTION OF NOTES

NOTES of a lexical and immediately explanatory character are usually printed at the foot of the page. Points requiring fuller explanation, together with other supplementary material, will be found at the back.

# FURTHER READING

Sargeaunt, M. J., *John Ford*, Oxford, 1935

Sensabaugh, G. F., *The Tragic Muse of John Ford*, Stanford and London, 1944

Ellis-Fermor, U. M., *The Jacobean Drama*, revised edition, 1958

Eliot, T. S., 'John Ford', in *Elizabethan Dramatists*, 1963

Ewing, B. S., *Burtonian Melancholy in the Plays of John Ford*, Princeton, 1940

Oliver, H. J., *The Problem of John Ford*, Melbourne, 1955

Sherman, S. P., 'Stella and *The Broken Heart*', *PMLA*, XXIV (1909), 274–85

Blayney, G. L., 'Convention, Plot, and Structure in *The Broken Heart*', *Modern Philology*, LVI (1958), 1–9

Kaufmann, R. J., 'Ford's Tragic Perspective', in *Elizabethan Drama*, ed. Kaufmann, New York and Oxford, 1961

Ure, P., 'Marriage and the Domestic Drama in Heywood and Ford', *English Studies*, XXXII (1951), 200–16

*Since 1980*

Anderson, Donald K, Jr, *'Concord in Discord': The Plays of John Ford, 1586–1986*, New York: AMS Press, 1986. Also: Hamilton, Sharon, '*The Broken Heart*: Language Suited to a Divided Mind', 171–193

Barton, Anne, 'Oxymoron and the Structure of Ford's *The Broken Heart*', *Essays and Studies* 33, 70–94

Dyer, William D., 'Holding/Withholding Environments: A Psychoanalytical Approach to Ford's *The Broken Heart*', *English Literary Renaissance* 21/3 (1991), 401–424

Ford, John, *Critical Re-visions*, ed. Michael Neill, Cambridge: CUP, 1988

*The Broken Heart*, ed T. J. B. Spencer, Manchester: MUP, 1980

Foster, Verna A., 'Structure and History in *The Broken Heart. Sparta, England and the "Truth",' English Literary Renaissance* 18/2 (1988), 305–328

Neill, Michael, 'Ford's Unbroken Art: The Moral Design of *The Broken Heart*', *The Modern Language Review* 75 (1980), no.2, 249–268

Padhi, Shanti, '*The Broken Heart* and *The Second's Maiden's Tragedy*: Ford's Main Source for the Corpse's Coronation', *Notes and Queries* 31/2 (1984), 236–7

Spinrad, Phoebe S., 'Ceremonies of Complement: The Symbolic Marriage in Ford's *The Broken Heart*', *Philological Quarterly* 65/1 (1986), 23–37

*The Selected Plays of John Ford*, ed. Colin Gibson, New York: CUP, 1986

# THE
# BROKEN HEART.

## A Tragedy.

*ACTED*
By the KINGS Majeſties Seruants
at the priuate Houſe in the
BLACK-FRIERS.

*Fide Honor.*

*LONDON:*
Printed by *I. B.* for HVGH BEESTON, and are to
be ſold at his Shop, neere the *Castle* in
*Corne-hill.* 1633.

R—B

## TO THE MOST WORTHY DESERVER OF THE NOBLEST TITLES IN HONOUR

William, Lord Craven, Baron of Hampstead-Marshall

MY LORD:

The glory of a great name, acquired by a greater glory of action, hath in all ages lived the truest chronicle to his own memory. In the practice of which argument, your growth to perfection (even in youth) hath appeared so sincere, so unflattering a penman, that posterity cannot with more delight read the merit of noble endeavours, than noble endeavours merit thanks from posterity to be read with delight. Many nations, many eyes, have been witnesses of your deserts, and loved them; be pleased, then, with the freedom of your own nature, to admit *one*, amongst all, particularly into the list of such as honour a fair example of nobility. There is a kind of humble ambition, not uncommendable, when the silence of study breaks forth into discourse, coveting rather encouragement than applause; yet herein censure commonly is too severe an auditor, without the moderation of an able patronage. I have ever been slow in courtship of greatness, not ignorant of such defects as are frequent to opinion; but the justice of your inclination to industry, emboldens my weakness of confidence to relish an experience of your mercy, as many brave dangers have tasted of your courage. Your lordship strove to be known to the world (when the world knew you least) by voluntary but excellent attempts: like allowance I plead of being known to your lordship (in this low presumption) by tendering, to a favourable entertainment, a devotion offered from a heart that can be as truly sensible of any least respect as ever profess the owner in my best, my readiest services, a lover of your natural love to virtue,

John Ford.

## The Scene

## SPARTA

The speakers' names, fitted to their qualities

| | |
|---|---|
| *Amyclas* | Common to the Kings of Laconia |
| *Ithocles*, Honour of loveliness, | A favourite |
| *Orgilus*, Angry, | Son to Crotolon |
| *Bassanes*, Vexation, | A jealous Nobleman |
| *Armostes*, An Appeaser, | A Counsellor of State |
| *Crotolon*, Noise, | Another Counsellor |
| *Prophilus*, Dear, | Friend to Ithocles |
| *Nearchus*, Young Prince, | Prince of Argos |
| *Tecnicus*, Artist, | A Philosopher |
| *Lemophil*, Glutton,<br>*Groneas*, Tavern-haunter, | Two Courtiers |
| *Amelus*, Trusty, | Friend to Nearchus |
| *Phulas*, Watchful, | Servant to Bassanes |
| *Calantha*, Flower of beauty, | The King's daughter |
| *Penthea*, Complaint, | Sister to Ithocles [and wife to Bassanes] |
| *Euphranea*, Joy, | A Maid of Honour [and daughter of Crotolon] |
| *Christalla*, Crystal,<br>*Philema*, A Kiss, | Maids of Honour |
| *Grausis*, Old Beldam, | Overseer of Penthea |

Persons Included

| | |
|---|---|
| *Thrasus*, Fierceness, | Father of Ithocles |
| *Aplotes*, Simplicity, | Orgilus so disguised |

## The Prologue

Our scene is Sparta. He whose best of art
Hath drawn this piece, calls it *The Broken Heart.*
The title lends no expectation here
Of apish laughter, or of some lame jeer
At place or persons; no pretended clause
Of jests fit for a brothel courts applause
From vulgar admiration: such low songs,
Tuned to unchaste ears, suit not modest tongues.
The virgin sisters then deserved fresh bays
When innocence and sweetness crowned their lays;
Then vices gasped for breath, whose whole commerce
Was whipped to exile by unblushing verse.
This law we keep in our presentment now,
Not to take freedom more than we allow;
What may be here thought a fiction, when time's youth
Wanted some riper years, was known a truth:
In which, if words have clothed the subject right,
You may partake a pity with delight.

5 *pretended clause of jests* group of stories offered
9 *virgin sisters* Muses
11 *commerce* trafficking
13 *presentment* presentation (the play)
15–16 (see p. 89)

## THE BROKEN HEART

### Act I, Scene i

*Enter* CROTOLON *and* ORGILUS

*Crotolon.* Dally not further, I will know the reason
That speeds thee to this journey.
*Orgilus.* Reason? good sir,
I can yield many.
*Crotolon.* Give me one, a good one;
Such I expect, and ere we part must have:
'Athens'? pray why to Athens? you intend not
To kick against the world, turn cynic, stoic,
Or read the logic lecture, or become
An Areopagite, and judge in causes
Touching the commonwealth? for, as I take it,
The budding of your chin cannot prognosticate
So grave an honour.
*Orgilus.* All this I acknowledge.
*Crotolon.* You do? then, son, if books and love of knowledge
Inflame you to this travel, here in Sparta
You may as freely study.
*Orgilus.* 'Tis not that, sir.
*Crotolon.* Not that, sir? As a father I command thee
To acquaint me with the truth.
*Orgilus.* Thus I obey 'ee.
After so many quarrels as dissension,
Fury, and rage had broached in blood, and sometimes
With death to such confederates as sided
With now dead Thrasus and yourself, my lord,
Our present king, Amyclas, reconciled
Your eager swords and sealed a gentle peace.
Friends you professed yourselves; which to confirm,
A resolution for a lasting league
Betwixt your families was entertained,
By joining in a Hymenean bond
Me and the fair Penthea, only daughter

7 *read the logic lecture* study logic
8 *Areopagite* member of the Athenian criminal court

To Thrasus.
*Crotolon.* What of this?
*Orgilus.* Much, much, dear sir.
A freedom of converse, an interchange
Of holy and chaste love, so fixed our souls
In a firm growth of union, that no time
Can eat into the pledge. We had enjoyed
The sweets our vows expected, had not cruelty
Prevented all those triumphs we prepared for
By Thrasus his untimely death.
*Crotolon.* Most certain.
*Orgilus.* From this time sprouted up that poisonous stalk
Of aconite, whose ripened fruit hath ravished
All health, all comfort of a happy life;
For Ithocles, her brother, proud of youth,
And prouder in his power, nourished closely
The memory of former discontents,
To glory in revenge. By cunning partly,
Partly by threats, 'a woos at once and forces
His virtuous sister to admit a marriage
With Bassanes, a nobleman, in honour
And riches, I confess, beyond my fortunes.
*Crotolon.* All this is no sound reason to importune
My leave for thy departure.
*Orgilus.* Now it follows.
Beauteous Penthea, wedded to this torture
By an insulting brother, being secretly
Compelled to yield her virgin freedom up
To him who never can usurp her heart,
Before contracted mine, is now so yoked
To a most barbarous thraldom, misery,
Affliction, that he savours not humanity,
Whose sorrow melts not into more than pity
In hearing but her name.
*Crotolon.* As how, pray?
*Orgilus.* Bassanes,
The man that calls her wife, considers truly
What heaven of perfections he is lord of
By thinking fair Penthea his. This thought
Begets a kind of monster-love, which love
Is nurse unto a fear so strong and servile

31 (see p. 89)
34 *triumphs* celebrations
37 *aconite* wolfsbane, or monk's hood
40 *closely* secretly
55 *he savours not humanity* he is less than human

As brands all dotage with a jealousy.
All eyes who gaze upon that shrine of beauty,
He doth resolve, do homage to the miracle;
Some one, he is assured, may now or then,
(If opportunity but sort) prevail.
So much, out of a self-unworthiness,
His fears transport him; not that he finds cause
In her obedience, but his own distrust.

*Crotolon.* You spin out your discourse.

*Orgilus.* My griefs are violent:
For knowing how the maid was heretofore
Courted by me, his jealousies grow wild
That I should steal again into her favours,
And undermine her virtues; which the gods
Know I nor dare nor dream of. Hence, from hence
I undertake a voluntary exile;
First, by my absence to take off the cares
Of jealous Bassanes; but chiefly, sir,
To free Penthea from a hell on earth;
Lastly, to lose the memory of something
Her presence makes to live in me afresh.

*Crotolon.* Enough, my Orgilus, enough. To Athens.
I give a full consent—alas good lady—
We shall hear from thee often?

*Orgilus.* Often.

*Crotolon.* See,
Thy sister comes to give a farewell.

*Enter* EUPHRANEA

*Euphranea.* Brother.

*Orgilus.* Euphranea, thus upon thy cheeks I print
A brother's kiss; more careful of thine honour,
Thy health, and thy well-doing, than my life.
Before we part, in presence of our father,
I must prefer a suit to 'ee.

*Euphranea.* You may style it,
My brother, a command.

*Orgilus.* That you will promise
To pass never to any man, however
Worthy, your faith, till, with our father's leave,
I give a free consent.

65 *resolve* conclude
67 *sort* present itself
91 *prefer a suit* make a request
94 (see p. 90)

*Crotolon.* An easy motion.
I'll promise for her, Orgilus.
*Orgilus.* Your pardon;
Euphranea's oath must yield me satisfaction.
*Euphranea.* By Vesta's sacred fires I swear.
*Crotolon.* And I,
By great Apollo's beams, join in the vow,
Not without thy allowance to bestow her
On any living.
*Orgilus.* Dear Euphranea,
Mistake me not; far, far 'tis from my thought,
As far from any wish of mine, to hinder
Preferment to an honourable bed
Or fitting fortune. Thou art young and handsome;
And 'twere injustice—more, a tyranny—
Not to advance thy merit. Trust me, sister,
It shall be my first care to see thee matched
As may become thy choice and our contents.
I have your oath.
*Euphranea.* You have. But mean you, brother,
To leave us, as you say?
*Crotolon.* Ay, ay, Euphranea.
He has just grounds direct him. I will prove
A father and a brother to thee.
*Euphranea.* Heaven
Does look into the secrets of all hearts.
Gods, you have mercy with 'ee, else—
*Crotolon.* Doubt nothing;
Thy brother will return in safety to us.
*Orgilus.* Souls sunk in sorrows never are without 'em;
They change fresh airs, but bear their griefs about 'em.
*Exeunt omnes*

## Act I, Scene ii

*Flourish. Enter* AMYCLAS *the King,* ARMOSTES, PROPHILUS, *and Attendants*

*Amyclas.* The Spartan gods are gracious; our humility
Shall bend before their altars, and perfume
Their temples with abundant sacrifice.
See, lords, Amyclas, your old king, is entering

95 *motion* proposal
98 (see p. 90)
100 *allowance* agreement
112 *direct* which direct
115 *Doubt* Fear

Into his youth again. I shall shake off
This silver badge of age, and change this snow
For hairs as gay as are Apollo's locks.
Our heart leaps in new vigour.

*Armostes.* May old time
Run back to double your long life, great sir.

*Amyclas.* It will, it must, Armostes. Thy bold nephew,
Death-braving Ithocles, brings to our gates
Triumphs and peace upon his conquering sword.
Laconia is a monarchy at length;
Hath in this latter war trod under foot
Messene's pride; Messene bows her neck
To Lacedemon's royalty. Oh, 'twas
A glorious victory, and doth deserve
More than a chronicle—a temple, lords,
A temple to the name of Ithocles.—
Where didst thou leave him, Prophilus?

*Prophilus.* At Pephon,
Most gracious sovereign; twenty of the noblest
Of the Messenians there attend your pleasure,
For such conditions as you shall propose
In settling peace, and liberty of life.

*Amyclas.* When comes your friend the general?

*Prophilus.* He promised
To follow with all speed convenient.

*Enter* CROTOLON, CALANTHA, EUPHRANEA, CHRISTALLA *and* PHILEMA [*with a garland*]

*Amyclas.* Our daughter! Dear Calantha, the happy news,
The conquest of Messene, hath already
Enriched thy knowledge.

*Calantha.* With the circumstance
And manner of the fight, related faithfully
By Prophilus himself—but, pray, sir, tell me,
How doth the youthful general demean
His actions in these fortunes?

*Prophilus.* Excellent princess,
Your own fair eyes may soon report a truth
Unto your judgement, with what moderation,
Calmness of nature, measure, bounds, and limits
Of thankfulness and joy, 'a doth digest
Such amplitude of his success as would
In others, moulded of a spirit less clear,

10–20 (see p. 90) 32 *demean* conduct

Advance 'em to comparison with heaven.
But Ithocles—
*Calantha.* Your friend—
*Prophilus.* He is so, madam,
In which the period of my fate consists:
He, in this firmament of honour, stands
Like a star fixed, not moved with any thunder
Of popular applause or sudden lightning
Of self-opinion. He hath served his country,
And thinks 'twas but his duty.
*Crotolon.* You describe
A miracle of man.
*Amyclas.* Such, Crotolon,
On forfeit of a king's word, thou wilt find him. [*Flourish*]
Hark, warning of his coming! All attend him.

*Enter* ITHOCLES, LEMOPHIL, *and* GRONEAS;
*the rest of the Lords ushering him in*

*Amyclas.* Return into these arms, thy home, thy sanctuary,
Delight of Sparta, treasure of my bosom,
Mine own, own Ithocles.
*Ithocles.* Your humblest subject.
*Armostes.* Proud of the blood I claim an interest in,
As brother to thy mother, I embrace thee
Right noble nephew.
*Ithocles.* Sir, your love's too partial.
*Crotolon.* Our country speaks by me, who by thy valour,
Wisdom, and service, shares in this great action;
Returning thee, in part of thy due merits,
A general welcome.
*Ithocles.* You exceed in bounty.
*Calantha.* Christalla, Philema, the chaplet.
[*Takes the chaplet from them*] Ithocles,
Upon the wings of Fame the singular
And chosen fortune of an high attempt
Is borne so past the view of common sight,
That I myself, with mine own hands, have wrought,
To crown thy temples, this provincial garland:
Accept, wear, and enjoy it as our gift
Deserved, not purchased.

42 *period* acme
59 *part* part payment
61 *chaplet* wreath for a victor's head
66 *provincial garland* awarded to the conqueror of a province (see also p. 90)

*Ithocles.* Y' are a royal maid.
*Amyclas.* She is in all our daughter.
*Ithocles.* Let me blush,
Acknowledging how poorly I have served,
What nothings I have done, compared with th' honours
Heaped on the issue of a willing mind;
In that lay mine ability, that only.
For who is he so sluggish from his birth,
So little worthy of a name or country,
That owes not out of gratitude for life
A debt of service, in what kind soever
Safety or counsel of the commonwealth
Requires, for payment?
*Calantha.* 'A speaks truth.
*Ithocles.* Whom heaven
Is pleased to style victorious, there, to such,
Applause runs madding, like the drunken priests
In Bacchus' sacrifices, without reason
Voicing the leader-on a demi-god;
Whenas, indeed, each common soldier's blood
Drops down as current coin in that hard purchase
As his whose much more delicate condition
Hath sucked the milk of ease. Judgement commands,
But resolution executes. I use not,
Before this royal presence, these fit slights
As in contempt of such as can direct;
My speech hath other end: not to attribute
All praise to one man's fortune, which is strengthed
By many hands. For instance, here is Prophilus,
A gentleman (I cannot flatter truth)
Of much desert; and, though in other rank,
Both Lemophil and Groneas were not missing
To wish their country's peace; for, in a word,
All there did strive their best, and 'twas our duty.
*Amyclas.* Courtiers turn soldiers! We vouchsafe our hand.
[LEMOPHIL *and* GRONEAS *kiss his hand*]
Observe your great example.
*Lemophil.* With all diligence.
*Groneas.* Obsequiously and hourly.
*Amyclas.* Some repose

71 *What nothings . . . mind* my intentions were good, but I have done nothing to deserve such honours
89 *fit slights* proper modesties 92 (see p. 90)
100 *Observe . . . example* model yourselves on Ithocles

After these toils are needful. We must think on
Conditions for the conquered; they expect 'em.
On,—Come, my Ithocles.
*Euphranea.* Sir, with your favour,
I need not a supporter.
*Prophilus.* Fate instructs me.
*Exeunt. Manent* LEMOPHIL, GRONEAS, CHRISTALLA *and* PHILEMA. LEMOPHIL *stays* CHRISTALLA, GRONEAS, PHILEMA.
*Christalla.* With me?
*Philema.* Indeed I dare not stay.
*Lemophil.* Sweet lady,
Soldiers are blunt,—your lip.
*Christalla.* Fie, this is rudeness;
You went not hence such creatures.
*Groneas.* Spirit of valour
Is of a mounting nature.
*Philema.* It appears so.
Pray, in earnest, how many men apiece
Have you two been the death of?
*Groneas.* 'Faith, not many;
We were composed of mercy.
*Lemophil.* For our daring,
You heard the general's approbation
Before the king.
*Christalla.* You 'wished your country's peace';
That showed your charity. Where are your spoils,
Such as the soldier fights for?
*Philema.* They are coming.
*Christalla.* By the next carrier, are they not?
*Groneas.* Sweet Philema,
When I was in the thickest of mine enemies,
Slashing off one man's head, another's nose,
Another's arms and legs—
*Philema.* And all together.
*Groneas.* Then would I with a sigh remember thee,
And cry 'Dear Philema, 'tis for thy sake
I do these deeds of wonder!'—Dost not love me
With all thy heart now?
*Philema.* Now as heretofore.
I have not put my love to use; the principal
Will hardly yield an interest.

105 (see p. 90) 111 *you* ed. yon Q
120 *all together* ed. altogether Q

*Groneas.* By Mars,
I'll marry thee.
*Philema.* By Vulcan, y' are forsworn,
Except my mind do alter strangely.
*Groneas.* One word.
*Christalla.* You lie beyond all modesty,—forbear me.
*Lemophil.* I'll make thee mistress of a city, 'tis
Mine own by conquest.
*Christalla.* By petition; sue for't
*In forma pauperis*—'City?' kennel. Gallants,
Off with your feathers, put on aprons, gallants;
Learn to reel, thrum, or trim a lady's dog,
And be good quiet souls of peace, hobgoblins.
*Lemophil.* Christalla!
*Christalla.* Practise to drill hogs, in hope
To share in the acorns. Soldiers? corncutters,
But not so valiant; they oft-times draw blood,
Which you durst never do. When you have practised
More wit, or more civility, we'll rank 'ee
I' th' list of men; till then, brave things-at-arms,
Dare not to speak to us,—most potent Groneas.
*Philema.* And Lemophil the hardy,—at your services.
*Groneas.* They scorn us as they did before we went.
*Lemophil.* Hang 'em, let us scorn them, and be revenged.
*Exeunt* CHRISTALLA *and* PHILEMA.
*Groneas.* Shall we?
*Lemophil.* We will; and when we slight them thus,
Instead of following them, they'll follow us.
It is a woman's nature.
*Groneas.* 'Tis a scurvy one.
*Exeunt omnes.*

## Act I, Scene iii

*Enter* TECNICUS, *a philosopher, and* ORGILUS
*disguised like a scholar of his.*

*Tecnicus.* Tempt not the stars, young man; thou canst not play

127 (see p. 90)
132 *kennel* Often 'gutter, drain', but here probably 'dog shelter'
132 (see p. 90)
133 *feathers* ed. Fathers Q
134 *reel* wind wool or silk
*thrum* make tufts in cloth

With the severity of fate. This change
Of habit, and disguise in outward view,
Hides not the secrets of thy soul within thee
From their quick-piercing eyes, which dive at all times
Down to thy thoughts. In thy aspect I note
A consequence of danger.

*Orgilus.* Give me leave,
Grave Tecnicus, without foredooming destiny,
Under thy roof to ease my silent griefs
By applying to my hidden wounds the balm
Of thy oraculous lectures. If my fortune
Run such a crooked by-way as to wrest
My steps to ruin, yet thy learned precepts
Shall call me back and set my footings straight.
I will not court the world.

*Tecnicus.* Ah, Orgilus,
Neglects in young men of delights, and life,
Run often to extremities; they care not
For harms to others, who contemn their own.

*Orgilus.* But I, most learned artist, am not so much
At odds with nature that I grutch the thrift
Of any true deserver; nor doth malice
Of present hopes so check them with despair
As that I yield to thought of more affliction
Than what is incident to frailty. Wherefore
Impute not this retired course of living
Some little time, to any other cause
Than what I justly render: the information
Of an unsettled mind, as the effect
Must clearly witness.

*Tecnicus.* Spirit of truth inspire thee.
On these conditions I conceal thy change,
And willingly admit thee for an auditor.
I'll to my study.

[*Exit* TECNICUS]

*Orgilus.* I to contemplations
In these delightful walks.—Thus metamorphosed
I may without suspicion hearken after
Penthea's usage and Euphranea's faith.

7 *consequence* inference, augury
8 *foredooming* prejudging
18 *contemn* despise
19 *artist* philosopher, scholar
20 *grutch* grudge
*thrift* success
21 *malice* discouragement
24 *frailty* human imperfection
27 *information* moulding of mind or character

Love, thou art full of mystery! The deities
Themselves are not secure in searching out
The secrets of those flames, which, hidden, waste
A breast made tributary to the laws
Of beauty. Physic yet hath never found
A remedy to cure a lover's wound.—
Ha! who are those that cross yon private walk
Into the shadowing grove, in amorous foldings?

PROPHILUS *passeth over, supporting* EUPHRANEA, *and whispering.*

My sister; oh, my sister! 'tis Euphranea
With Prophilus; supported too. I would
It were an apparition. Prophilus
Is Ithocles his friend. It strangely puzzles me—

*Enter again* PROPHILUS *and* EUPHRANEA.

Again? help me, my book; this scholar's habit
Must stand my privilege: my mind is busy,
Mine eyes and ears are open.

*Walks by, reading.*

*Prophilus.* Do not waste
The span of this stolen time (lent by the gods
For precious use) in niceness. Bright Euphranea,
Should I repeat old vows, or study new,
For purchase of belief to my desires,—
*Orgilus.* Desires?
*Prophilus.* My service, my integrity,—
*Orgilus.* That's better.
*Prophilus.* I should but repeat a lesson
Oft conned without a prompter, but thine eyes.
My love is honourable,—
*Orgilus.* So was mine
To my Penthea, chastely honourable.
*Prophilus.* Nor wants there more addition to my wish
Of happiness than having thee a wife;
Already sure of Ithocles, a friend
Firm and unalterable.
*Orgilus.* But a brother
More cruel than the grave.
*Euphranea.* What can you look for,
In answer to your noble protestations,
From an unskilful maid, but language suited
To a divided mind?

43 *foldings* embraces
44 (see p. 91)
50 s.d. *Walks* ed. walke Q
52 *niceness* coyness

*Orgilus.* Hold out, Euphranea.
*Euphranea.* Know, Prophilus, I never undervalued
(From the first time you mentioned worthy love)
Your merit, means, or person. It had been
A fault of judgement in me, and a dulness
In my affections, not to weigh and thank
My better stars that offered me the grace
Of so much blissfulness. For, to speak truth,
The law of my desires kept equal pace
With yours, nor have I left that resolution;
But only, in a word, whatever choice
Lives nearest in my heart, must first procure
Consent both from my father and my brother,
Ere he can own me his.
*Orgilus.* She is forsworn else.
*Prophilus.* Leave me that task.
*Euphranea.* My brother, ere he parted
To Athens, had my oath.
*Orgilus.* Yes, yes, 'a had, sure.
*Prophilus.* I doubt not, with the means the court supplies,
But to prevail at pleasure.
*Orgilus.* Very likely.
*Prophilus.* Meantime, best, dearest, I may build my
hopes
On the foundation of thy constant sufferance
In any opposition.
*Euphranea.* Death shall sooner
Divorce life and the joys I have in living
Than my chaste vows from truth.
*Prophilus.* On thy fair hand
I seal the like.
*Orgilus.* There is no faith in woman.
Passion, oh be contained: my very heart-strings
Are on the tenters.
*Euphranea.* Sir, we are overheard.
Cupid protect us! 'Twas a stirring, sir,
Of someone near.
*Prophilus.* Your fears are needless, lady.
None have access into these private pleasures
Except some near in court, or bosom student
From Tecnicus his oratory, granted
By special favour lately from the king

77 *choice* chosen lover 86 *constant sufferance* faithfulness
92 *tenters* hooks for stretching cloth
97 *oratory* place for public speaking, school

Unto the grave philosopher.
*Euphranea.* Methinks
I hear one talking to himself—I see him.
*Prophilus.* 'Tis a poor scholar, as I told you, lady.
*Orgilus.* I am discovered—[*As if thinking aloud*]
Say it: is it possible,
With a smooth tongue, a leering countenance,
Flattery, or force of reason—(I come t'ee, sir)
To turn or to appease the raging sea?
Answer to that.—Your art? what art to catch
And hold fast in a net the sun's small atoms?
No, no; they'll out, they'll out; ye may as easily
Outrun a cloud driven by a northern blast
As fiddle-faddle so. Peace, or speak sense.
*Euphranea.* Call you this thing a scholar? 'Las, he's lunatic.
*Prophilus.* Observe him, sweet; 'tis but his recreation.
*Orgilus.* But will you hear a little! You are so tetchy,
You keep no rule in argument. Philosophy
Works not upon impossibilities,
But natural conclusions.—Mew!—absurd!
The metaphysics are but speculations
Of the celestial bodies, or such accidents
As not mixed perfectly, in the air engendered,
Appear to us unnatural; that's all.
Prove it.—Yet, with a reverence to your gravity,
I'll balk illiterate sauciness, submitting
My sole opinion to the touch of writers.
*Prophilus.* Now let us fall in with him.
*Orgilus.* Ha, ha, ha!
These apish boys, when they but taste the grammates
And principles of theory, imagine
They can oppose their teachers. Confidence
Leads many into errors.
*Prophilus.* By your leave, sir.
*Euphranea.* Are you a scholar, friend?
*Orgilus.* I am, gay creature,
With pardon of your deities, a mushroom
On whom the dew of heaven drops now and then.
The sun shines on me too, I thank his beams;
Sometime I feel their warmth, and eat, and sleep.
*Prophilus.* Does Tecnicus read to thee?

102–23 (see p. 91) 123 *touch of writers* test by authorities
125 *grammates* rudiments (O.E.D. cites only this instance)
134 *read to thee* teach you

*Orgilus.* Yes, forsooth,
He is my master surely; yonder door
Opens upon his study.
*Prophilus.* Happy creatures.
Such people toil not, sweet, in heats of state,
Nor sink in thaws of greatness; their affections
Keep order with the limits of their modesty;
Their love is love of virtue.—What's thy name?
*Orgilus.* Aplotes, sumptuous master, a poor wretch.
*Euphranea.* Dost thou want anything?
*Orgilus.* Books, Venus, books.
*Prophilus.* Lady, a new conceit comes in my thought,
And most available for both our comforts.
*Euphranea.* My lord,—
*Prophilus.* Whiles I endeavour to deserve
Your father's blessing to our loves, this scholar
May daily at some certain hours attend
What notice I can write of my success,
Here in this grove, and give it to your hands;
The like from you to me: so can we never,
Barred of our mutual speech, want sure intelligence;
And thus our hearts may talk when our tongues cannot.
*Euphranea.* Occasion is most favourable; use it.
*Prophilus.* Aplotes, wilt thou wait us twice a day,
At nine i' th' morning and at four at night,
Here in this bower, to convey such letters
As each shall send to other? Do it willingly,
Safely, and secretly, and I will furnish
Thy study, or what else thou canst desire.
*Orgilus.* Jove, make me thankful, thankful, I beseech thee,
Propitious Jove. I will prove sure and trusty.
You will not fail me books?
*Prophilus.* Nor aught besides
Thy heart can wish. This lady's name's Euphranea,
Mine Prophilus.
*Orgilus.* I have a pretty memory;
It must prove my best friend.—I will not miss
One minute of the hours appointed.
*Prophilus.* Write
The books thou wouldst have bought thee in a note,
Or take thyself some money.
*Orgilus.* No, no money.

143 *conceit* idea
151 *sure intelligence* reliable information

Money to scholars is a spirit invisible,
We dare not finger it: or books, or nothing.

*Prophilus.* Books of what sort thou wilt: do not forget
Our names.

*Orgilus.* I warrant 'ee, I warrant 'ee.

*Prophilus.* Smile, Hymen, on the growth of our desires;
We'll feed thy torches with eternal fires.

*Exeunt. Manet* ORGILUS

*Orgilus.* Put out thy torches, Hymen, or their light
Shall meet a darkness of eternal night.
Inspire me, Mercury, with swift deceits.
Ingenious Fate has leapt into mine arms,
Beyond the compass of my brain. Mortality
Creeps on the dung of earth, and cannot reach
The riddles which are purposed by the gods.
Great arts best write themselves in their own stories;
They die too basely who outlive their glories.

*Exit.*

## Act II, Scene i

*Enter* BASSANES *and* PHULAS

*Bassanes.* I'll have that window next the street dammed
up;
It gives too full a prospect to temptation,
And courts a gazer's glances. There's a lust
Committed by the eye, that sweats and travails,
Plots, wakes, contrives, till the deformed bear-whelp
Adultery be licked into the act,
The very act. That light shall be dammed up;
D' ee hear, sir?

*Phulas.* I do hear, my lord; a mason
Shall be provided suddenly.

*Bassanes.* Some rogue,
Some rogue of your confederacy, (factor
For slaves and strumpets) to convey close packets
From this spruce springal and the tother youngster,
That gaudy earwig, or my lord your patron,

180 *reach* comprehend
7 *light* window
10 *factor* agent
12 *springal* youth

1 (see p. 91)
9 *suddenly* immediately
11 *close packets* secret letters
13 *earwig* flatterer

Whose pensioner you are.—I'll tear thy throat out,
Son of a cat, ill-looking hound's-head, rip up
Thy ulcerous maw, if I but scent a paper,
A scroll, but half as big as what can cover
A wart upon thy nose, a spot, a pimple,
Directed to my lady. It may prove
A mystical preparative to lewdness.
*Phulas.* Care shall be had.—I will turn every thread
About me to an eye.—Here's a sweet life.
*Bassanes.* The city housewives, cunning in the traffic
Of chamber-merchandise, set all at price
By wholesale; yet they wipe their mouths and simper,
Cull, kiss, and cry 'sweetheart', and stroke the head
Which they have branched; and all is well again.
Dull clods of dirt, who dare not feel the rubs
Stuck on their foreheads.
*Phulas.* 'Tis a villainous world;
One cannot hold his own in't.
*Bassanes.* Dames at court,
Who flaunt in riots, run another bias.
Their pleasure heaves the patient ass that suffers
Up on the stilts of office, titles, incomes;
Promotion justifies the shame, and sues for't.
Poor honour, thou art stabbed, and bleedest to death
By such unlawful hire. The country mistress
Is yet more wary, and in blushes hides
Whatever trespass draws her troth to guilt.
But all are false. On this truth I am bold:
No woman but can fall, and doth, or would.—
Now for the newest news about the city;
What blab the voices, sirrah?
*Phulas.* Oh, my lord,
The rarest, quaintest, strangest, tickling news
That ever—
*Bassanes.* Hey-day! up and ride me, rascal!
What is 't?
*Phulas.* Forsooth, they say the king has mewed
All his grey beard, instead of which is budded
Another of a pure carnation colour,
Speckled with green and russet.

20 *mystical* secret
23 *housewives* hussies
26 *Cull* embrace
27 *branched* horned
29 *their* ed. the Q
31 *bias* indirect course
41 (see p. 91)
45 *mewed* shed (used of a bird moulting)

*Bassanes.* Ignorant block!
*Phulas.* Yes, truly; and 'tis talked about the streets
That since Lord Ithocles came home, the lions
Never left roaring, at which noise the bears
Have danced their very hearts out.
*Bassanes.* Dance out thine too.
*Phulas.* Besides, Lord Orgilus is fled to Athens
Upon a fiery dragon, and 'tis thought
'A never can return.
*Bassanes.* Grant it, Apollo!
*Phulas.* Moreover, please your lordship, 'tis reported
For certain, that whoever is found jealous,
Without apparent proof that 's wife is wanton,
Shall be divorced; but this is but she-news,
I had it from a midwife. I have more yet.
*Bassanes.* Antic, no more. Idiots and stupid fools
Grate my calamities. Why, to be fair
Should yield presumption of a faulty soul—
Look to the doors.
*Phulas.* The horn of plenty crest him.
*Exit* PHULAS
*Bassanes.* Swarms of confusion huddle in my thoughts
In rare distemper. Beauty! Oh, it is
An unmatched blessing, or a horrid curse.

*Enter* PENTHEA *and* GRAUSIS, *an old Lady*

She comes, she comes. So shoots the morning forth,
Spangled with pearls of transparent dew.
The way to poverty is to be rich,
As I in her am wealthy; but for her,
In all contents a bankrupt.—Loved Penthea,
How fares my heart's best joy?
*Grausis.* In sooth, not well;
She is so over-sad.
*Bassanes.* Leave chattering, magpie.—
Thy brother is returned, sweet, safe, and honoured
With a triumphant victory: thou shalt visit him.
We will to court, where, if it be thy pleasure,
Thou shalt appear in such a ravishing lustre

61 *Antic* Fool
64 *The horn . . . him* may his miserliness make him a cuckold
67 s.d. *Grausis* here and often in Q Gransis
69 (see p. 91)

Of jewels above value, that the dames
Who brave it there, in rage to be outshined,
Shall hide them in their closets, and unseen
Fret in their tears; whiles every wondering eye
Shall crave none other brightness but thy presence.
Choose thine own recreations, be a queen
Of what delights thou fanciest best, what company,
What place, what times. Do anything, do all things
Youth can command, so thou wilt chase these clouds
From the pure firmament of thy fair looks.
*Grausis.* Now 'tis well said, my lord. What, lady! laugh,
Be merry; time is precious.
*Bassanes.* [*Aside*] Furies whip thee.
*Penthea.* Alas, my lord, this language to your handmaid
Sounds as would music to the deaf. I need
No braveries nor cost of art, to draw
The whiteness of my name into offence.
Let such (if any such there are) who covet
A curiosity of admiration,
By laying out their plenty to full view,
Appear in gaudy outsides; my attires
Shall suit the inward fashion of my mind;
From which, if your opinion, nobly placed,
Change not the livery your words bestow,
My fortunes with my hopes are at the highest.
*Bassanes.* This house, methinks, stands somewhat too much inward,
It is too melancholy; we'll remove
Nearer the court: or what thinks my Penthea
Of the delightful island we command?
Rule me as thou canst wish.
*Penthea.* I am no mistress.
Whither you please, I must attend; all ways
Are alike pleasant to me.
*Grausis.* Island? prison!
A prison is as gaysome. We'll no islands.
Marry, out upon 'em! Whom shall we see there?
Sea-gulls, and porpoises, and water-rats,
And crabs, and mews, and dogfish; goodly gear
For a young lady's dealing,—or an old one's.
On no terms islands. I'll be stewed first.

96 An excessive care for the admiration of others
98 *outsides* trappings 101 *livery* privilege of service
113 *mews* seagulls

*Bassanes.* [*Aside to* GRAUSIS] Grausis,
You are a juggling bawd.—This sadness, sweetest,
Becomes not youthful blood. [*Aside to* GRAUSIS] I'll have
you pounded.
For my sake put on a more cheerful mirth;
Thou't mar thy cheeks, and make me old in griefs.—
[*Aside to* GRAUSIS] Damnable bitch-fox.
*Grausis.* I am thick of hearing,
Still, when the wind blows southerly.—What think 'ee
If your fresh lady breed young bones, my lord?
Would not a chopping boy d'ee good at heart?
But, as you said—
*Bassanes.* [*Aside to* GRAUSIS] I'll spit thee on a stake,
Or chop thee into collops.
*Grausis.* Pray, speak louder.
Sure, sure, the wind blows south still.
*Penthea.* Thou pratest madly.
*Bassanes.* 'Tis very hot; I sweat extremely.

*Enter* PHULAS

Now?
*Phulas.* A herd of lords, sir.
*Bassanes.* Ha!
*Phulas.* A flock of ladies.
*Bassanes.* Where?
*Phulas.* Shoals of horses.
*Bassanes.* Peasant, how?
*Phulas.* Caroches
In drifts—th' one enter, th' other stand without, sir.
And now I vanish.

*Exit* PHULAS

*Enter* PROPHILUS, LEMOPHIL, GRONEAS, CHRISTALLA *and* PHILEMA

*Prophilus.* Noble Bassanes.
*Bassanes.* Most welcome, Prophilus. Ladies, gentlemen,
To all, my heart is open; you all honour me,—
(A tympany swells in my head already)
Honour me bountifully.—(How they flutter,
Wagtails and jays together).
*Prophilus.* From your brother,

121 *Still* always
123 *chopping* strapping
125 *collops* chunks of meat
129 *Caroches* luxurious coaches
134 *tympany* tumour (often associated with pride or jealousy)

By virtue of your love to him, I require
Your instant presence, fairest.
*Penthea.* He is well, sir?
*Prophilus.* The gods preserve him ever. Yet, dear beauty,
I find some alteration in him lately,
Since his return to Sparta. My good lord,
I pray, use no delay.
*Bassanes.* We had not needed
An invitation, if his sister's health
Had not fallen into question.—Haste, Penthea,
Slack not a minute. Lead the way, good Prophilus;
I'll follow step by step.
*Prophilus.* Your arm, fair madam.

*Exeunt all but* BASSANES *and* GRAUSIS

*Bassanes.* One word with your old bawdship: th' hadst been better
Railed at the sins thou worshipp'st than have thwarted
My will. I'll use thee cursedly.
*Grausis.* You dote,
You are beside yourself. A politician
In jealousy? No, y' are too gross, too vulgar.
Pish, teach not me my trade; I know my cue.
My crossing you sinks me into her trust,
By which I shall know all: my trade's a sure one.
*Bassanes.* Forgive me, Grausis, 'twas consideration
I relished not; but have a care now.
*Grausis.* Fear not,
I am no new-come-to't.
*Bassanes.* Thy life's upon it,
And so is mine. My agonies are infinite.

*Exeunt omnes*

## Act II, Scene ii

*Enter* ITHOCLES, *alone*

*Ithocles.* Ambition! 'tis of vipers' breed: it gnaws
A passage through the womb that gave it motion.

147–8 *th' hadst . . . worshipp'st* you would have been better off blaspheming against the vices you honour and serve (see also p. 91)
150 *politician* schemer
155–6 *'twas . . . not* that's a point I hadn't thought of
1–2 (see p. 91)

Ambition, like a seeled dove, mounts upward,
Higher and higher still, to perch on clouds,
But tumbles headlong down with heavier ruin.
So squibs and crackers fly into the air,
Then, only breaking with a noise, they vanish
In stench and smoke. Morality, applied
To timely practice, keeps the soul in tune,
At whose sweet music all our actions dance.
But this is form of books, and school-tradition;
It physics not the sickness of a mind
Broken with griefs: strong fevers are not eased
With counsel, but with best receipts, and means.
Means, speedy means, and certain; that's the cure.

*Enter* ARMOSTES *and* CROTOLON

*Armostes.* You stick, Lord Crotolon, upon a point
Too nice, and too unnecessary; Prophilus
Is every way desertful. I am confident
Your wisdom is too ripe to need instruction
From your son's tutelage.
*Crotolon.* Yet not so ripe,
My Lord Armostes, that it dares to dote
Upon the painted meat of smooth persuasion,
Which tempts me to a breach of faith.
*Ithocles.* Not yet
Resolved, my lord? Why, if your son's consent
Be so available, we'll write to Athens
For his repair to Sparta. The king's hand
Will join with our desires; he has been moved to 't.
*Armostes.* Yes, and the king himself importuned Crotolon
For a dispatch.
*Crotolon.* Kings may command; their wills
Are laws not to be questioned.
*Ithocles.* By this marriage
You knit an union so devout, so hearty,
Between your loves to me and mine to yours,
As if mine own blood had an interest in it;

3 *seeled* with its eyes sewn up
9 *timely practice* present business
11 *form of books* textbook procedure
*school-tradition* pedantry
14 *receipts* recipes, prescriptions for action
17 *nice* finicky
22 *painted meat* bait
25 *available* capable of producing a desired result

For Prophilus is mine, and I am his.
*Crotolon.* My lord, my lord,—
*Ithocles.* What, good sir? Speak your thought.
*Crotolon.* Had this sincerity been real once,
My Orgilus had not been now unwived,
Nor your lost sister buried in a bride-bed.
Your uncle here, Armostes, knows this truth;
For had your father Thrasus lived,—but peace
Dwell in his grave. I have done.
*Armostes.* Y' are bold and bitter.
*Ithocles.* 'A presses home the injury; it smarts.—
No reprehensions, uncle; I deserve 'em.
Yet, gentle sir, consider what the heat
Of an unsteady youth, a giddy brain,
Green indiscretion, flattery of greatness,
Rawness of judgement, wilfulness in folly,
Thoughts vagrant as the wind, and as uncertain,
Might lead a boy in years to. 'Twas a fault,
A capital fault; for then I could not dive
Into the secrets of commanding love;
Since when, experience by the extremities in others
Hath forced me to collect. And, trust me, Crotolon,
I will redeem those wrongs with any service
Your satisfaction can require for current.
*Armostes.* Thy acknowledgement is satisfaction.—
What would you more?
*Crotolon.* I'm conquered. If Euphranea
Herself admit the motion, let it be so.
I doubt not my son's liking.
*Ithocles.* Use my fortunes,
Life, power, sword, and heart,—all are your own.

*Enter* BASSANES, PROPHILUS, CALANTHA, PENTHEA, EUPHRANEA, CHRISTALLA, PHILEMA, *and* GRAUSIS

*Armostes.* The princess, with your sister.
*Calantha.* I present 'ee
A stranger here in court, my lord; for did not
Desire of seeing you draw her abroad,
We had not been made happy in her company.
*Ithocles.* You are a gracious princess.—Sister, wedlock
Holds too severe a passion in your nature,

50 *capital* deadly
53 *collect* form a conclusion, draw an inference
55 *current* present value 58 *admit* accept

Which can engross all duty to your husband,
Without attendance on so dear a mistress.—
'Tis not my brother's pleasure, I presume,
T' immure her in a chamber.
*Bassanes.* 'Tis her will;
She governs her own hours. Noble Ithocles,
We thank the gods for your success and welfare.
Our lady has of late been indisposed,
Else we had waited on you with the first.
*Ithocles.* How does Penthea now?
*Penthea.* You best know, brother,
From whom my health and comforts are derived.
*Bassanes.* [*Aside*] I like the answer well; 'tis sad and modest.
There may be tricks yet, tricks.—Have an eye, Grausis.
*Calantha.* Now, Crotolon, the suit we joined in must not
Fall by too long demur.
*Crotolon.* 'Tis granted, princess,
For my part.
*Armostes.* With condition, that his son
Favour the contract.
*Calantha.* Such delay is easy.—
The joys of marriage make thee, Prophilus,
A proud deserver of Euphranea's love,
And her of thy desert.
*Prophilus.* Most sweetly gracious.
*Bassanes.* The joys of marriage are the heaven on earth,
Life's paradise, great princess, the soul's quiet,
Sinews of concord, earthly immortality,
Eternity of pleasures;—no restoratives
Like to a constant woman. [*Aside*] But where is she?
'Twould puzzle all the gods but to create
Such a new monster.—I can speak by proof,
For I rest in Elysium; 'tis my happiness.
*Crotolon.* Euphranea, how are you resolved, speak freely,
In your affections to this gentleman?
*Euphranea.* Nor more, nor less than as his love assures me;
Which (if your liking with my brother's warrants)
I cannot but approve in all points worthy.
*Crotolon.* So, so. I know your answer.

77 *sad* serious

*Ithocles.* 'T had been pity
To sunder hearts so equally consented.

*Enter* LEMOPHIL

*Lemophil.* The king, Lord Ithocles, commands your presence,—
And, fairest princess, yours.
*Calantha.* We will attend him.

*Enter* GRONEAS

*Groneas.* Where are the lords? All must unto the king
Without delay. The Prince of Argos—
*Calantha.* Well, sir?
*Groneas.* Is coming to the court, sweet lady.
*Calantha.* How!
The Prince of Argos?
*Groneas.* 'Twas my fortune, madam,
T' enjoy the honour of these happy tidings.
*Ithocles.* Penthea!
*Penthea.* Brother?
*Ithocles.* Let me an hour hence
Meet you alone, within the palace grove;
I have some secret with you.—[*To* PROPHILUS] Prithee, friend,
Conduct her thither, and have special care
The walks be cleared of any to disturb us.
*Prophilus.* I shall.
*Bassanes.* [*Aside*] How's that?
*Ithocles.* Alone, pray be alone.—
I am your creature, princess.—On, my lords.
*Exeunt.* [*Manet*] BASSANES.
*Bassanes.* Alone. Alone? What means that word 'alone'?
Why might not I be there?—hum!—he's her brother.
Brothers and sisters are but flesh and blood,
And this same whoreson court-ease is temptation
To a rebellion in the veins.—Besides,
His fine friend Prophilus must be her guardian.
Why may not he dispatch a business nimbly
Before the other come?—or—pandering, pandering
For one another (be't to sister, mother,
Wife, cousin, anything) 'mongst youths of mettle
Is in request. It is so—stubborn fate!

104 (see p. 91)
115–27 (see p. 91)
125 *in request* fashionable

But if I be a cuckold, and can know it,
I will be fell, and fell.

*Enter* GRONEAS

*Groneas.* My lord, y'are called for.
*Bassanes.* Most heartily I thank ye. Where's my wife,
pray?
*Groneas.* Retired amongst the ladies.
*Bassanes.* Still I thank 'ee.
There's an old waiter with her; saw you her too?
*Groneas.* She sits i' th' presence-lobby fast asleep, sir.
*Bassanes.* Asleep? sleep, sir?
*Groneas.* Is your lordship troubled?
You will not to the king?
*Bassanes.* Your humblest vassal.
*Groneas.* Your servant, my good lord.
*Bassanes.* I wait your footsteps.
*Exeunt.*

## Act II, Scene iii

PROPHILUS, PENTHEA.

*Prophilus.* In this walk, lady, will your brother find you:
And, with your favour, give me leave a little
To work a preparation. In his fashion
I have observed of late some kind of slackness
To such alacrity as nature once
And custom took delight in. Sadness grows
Upon his recreations, which he hoards
In such a willing silence, that to question
The grounds will argue little skill in friendship,
And less good manners.
*Penthea.* Sir, I'm not inquisitive
Of secrecies without an invitation.
*Prophilus.* With pardon, lady, not a syllable
Of mine implies so rude a sense; the drift—

*Enter* ORGILUS [*disguised as before*]

127 *fell* cruel
134 *wait* attend
5 *once* ed. not in Q
9 *little* ed. not in Q
130 *waiter* attendant
3 *fashion* way of life
8 *willing* determined

[*To* ORGILUS] Do thy best
To make this lady merry for an hour.

*Exit.*

*Orgilus.* Your will shall be a law, sir.
*Penthea.* Prithee, leave me.
I have some private thoughts I would account with:
Use thou thine own.
*Orgilus.* Speak on, fair nymph; our souls
Can dance as well to music of the spheres
As any's who have feasted with the gods.
*Penthea.* Your school-terms are too troublesome.
*Orgilus.* What heaven
Refines mortality from dross of earth,
But such as uncompounded beauty hallows
With glorified perfection?
*Penthea.* Set thy wits
In a less wild proportion.
*Orgilus.* Time can never
On the white table of unguilty faith
Write counterfeit dishonour; turn those eyes
(The arrows of pure love) upon that fire
Which once rose to a flame, perfumed with vows
As sweetly scented as the incense smoking
On Vesta's altars—virgin tears (like
The holiest odours) sprinkled dews to feed 'em,
And to increase their fervour.
*Penthea.* Be not frantic.
*Orgilus.* All pleasures are but mere imagination,
Feeding the hungry appetite with steam
And sight of banquet, whilst the body pines,
Not relishing the real taste of food:
Such is the leanness of a heart divided
From intercourse of troth-contracted loves.
No horror should deface that precious figure
Sealed with the lively stamp of equal souls.
*Penthea.* Away! some fury hath bewitched thy tongue.
The breath of ignorance, that flies from thence,
Ripens a knowledge in me of afflictions

21 *school-terms* scholastic jargon (see also p. 91)
21–4 (see p. 91)
23 *uncompounded* pure, unmixed
25 *proportion* order, harmony
30–3 (see p. 92)
34 *mere* pure
41 *equal* equally consenting (cf. II.ii, 100)

Above all sufferance.—Thing of talk, begone,
Begone, without reply.
*Orgilus.* Be just, Penthea,
In thy commands: when thou sendest forth a doom
Of banishment, know first on whom it lights.
Thus I take off the shroud, in which my cares
Are folded up from view of common eyes.
[*Removes his scholar's gown*]
What is thy sentence next?
*Penthea.* Rash man. Thou layest
A blemish on mine honour, with the hazard
Of thy too desperate life. Yet I profess,
By all the laws of ceremonious wedlock,
I have not given admittance to one thought
Of female change since cruelty enforced
Divorce betwixt my body and my heart.
Why would you fall from goodness thus?
*Orgilus.* Oh, rather
Examine me how I could live to say
I have been much, much wronged. 'Tis for thy sake
I put on this imposture. Dear Penthea,
If thy soft bosom be not turned to marble,
Thou't pity our calamities; my interest
Confirms me thou art mine still.
*Penthea.* Lend your hand.
With both of mine I clasp it thus, thus kiss it,
Thus kneel before ye.
*Orgilus.* You instruct my duty.
*Penthea.* We may stand up. Have you aught else to urge
Of new demand? As for the old, forget it;
'Tis buried in an everlasting silence,
And shall be, shall be ever. What more would ye?
*Orgilus.* I would possess my wife; the equity
Of very reason bids me.
*Penthea.* Is that all?
*Orgilus.* Why, 'tis the all of me, myself.
*Penthea.* Remove
Your steps some distance from me:—at this space
A few words I dare change; but first put on
Your borrowed shape.
*Orgilus.* You are obeyed; 'tis done.
[*Resumes his disguise*]

63 *interest* right or title 64 *Confirms* assures
66 *instruct my duty* teach me what I should do

*Penthea.* How, Orgilus, by promise I was thine
The heavens do witness: they can witness too
A rape done on my truth. How I do love thee
Yet, Orgilus, and yet, must best appear
In tendering thy freedom; for I find
The constant preservation of thy merit,
By thy not daring to attempt my fame
With injury of any loose conceit,
Which might give deeper wounds to discontents.
Continue this fair race; then, though I cannot
Add to thy comfort, yet I shall more often
Remember from what fortune I am fallen,
And pity mine own ruin. Live, live happy,
Happy in thy next choice, that thou mayest people
This barren age with virtues in thy issue.
And, oh, when thou art married, think on me
With mercy, not contempt. I hope thy wife,
Hearing my story, will not scorn my fall.
Now let us part.
*Orgilus.* Part? Yet advise thee better:
Penthea is the wife to Orgilus,
And ever shall be.
*Penthea.* Never shall nor will.
*Orgilus.* How!
*Penthea.* Hear me; in a word I'll tell thee why.
The virgin-dowry which my birth bestowed
Is ravished by another; my true love
Abhors to think that Orgilus deserved
No better favours than a second bed.
*Orgilus.* I must not take this reason.
*Penthea.* To confirm it,
Should I outlive my bondage, let me meet
Another worse than this, and less desired,
If, of all men alive, thou shouldst but touch
My lip or hand again.
*Orgilus.* Penthea, now
I tell 'ee, you grow wanton in my sufferance.
Come, sweet, th' art mine.
*Penthea.* Uncivil sir, forbear,

81 *tendering* cherishing
83 *attempt my fame* attack my honour
84 *loose conceit* wild idea 86 *race* course of action
106 *all men* ed. all the men Q
108 *grow . . . sufferance* abuse my patience

Or I can turn affection into vengeance;
Your reputation (if you value any)
Lies bleeding at my feet. Unworthy man,
If ever henceforth thou appear in language,
Message, or letter, to betray my frailty,
I'll call thy former protestations lust,
And curse my stars for forfeit of my judgement.
Go thou, fit only for disguise and walks,
To hide thy shame; this once I spare thy life.
I laugh at mine own confidence; my sorrows
By thee are made inferior to my fortunes.
If ever thou didst harbour worthy love,
Dare not to answer. My good genius guide me,
That I may never see thee more.—Go from me.

*Orgilus.* I'll tear my veil of politic frenzy off,
And stand up like a man resolved to do:
Action, not words, shall show me. Oh, Penthea!

*Exit* ORGILUS

*Penthea.* 'A sighed my name, sure, as he parted from me;
I fear I was too rough. Alas, poor gentleman.
'A looked not like the ruins of his youth,
But like the ruins of those ruins. Honour,
How much we fight with weakness to preserve thee.

*Enter* BASSANES *and* GRAUSIS

*Bassanes.* Fie on thee! Damn thee, rotten maggot, damn thee!
Sleep? sleep at court? and now? Aches, convulsions,
Imposthumes, rheums, gouts, palsies, clog thy bones
A dozen years more yet.

*Grausis.* Now y' are in humours.

*Bassanes.* She's by herself, there's hope of that; she's sad too;
She's in strong contemplation; yes, and fixed:
The signs are wholesome.

*Grausis.* Very wholesome, truly.

116 *for . . . judgement* for misguiding me into loving you
122 *good genius* used here in the sense of 'good angel'
124 *politic frenzy* assumed madness (politicke French Q). (see also p. 92)
126 *show me* demonstrate what I am
133 *Aches* pronounced 'aitches', like the plural of 'h'
134 *Imposthumes* abscesses 135 *in humours* displeased
137 *fixed* composed, abstracted

*Bassanes*. Hold your chops, nightmare.—Lady, come; your brother
Is carried to his closet; you must thither.
*Penthea*. Not well, my lord?
*Bassanes*. A sudden fit, 'twill off;
Some surfeit or disorder.—How dost, dearest?
*Penthea*. Your news is none o' th' best.

*Enter* PROPHILUS

*Prophilus*. The chief of men,
The excellentest Ithocles, desires
Your presence, madam.
*Bassanes*. We are hasting to him.
*Penthea*. In vain we labour in this course of life
To piece our journey out at length, or crave
Respite of breath: our home is in the grave.
*Bassanes*. Perfect philosophy.
*Penthea*. Then let us care
To live so, that our reckonings may fall even
When w' are to make account.
*Prophilus*. He cannot fear
Who builds on noble grounds; sickness or pain
Is the deserver's exercise, and such
Your virtuous brother to the world is known.
Speak comfort to him, lady, be all gentle;
Stars fall but in the grossness of our sight;
A good man dying, th' earth doth lose a light.

*Exeunt omnes.*

## Act III, Scene i

*Enter* TECNICUS, *and* ORGILUS *in his own shape*

*Tecnicus*. Be well advised; let not a resolution
Of giddy rashness choke the breath of reason.
*Orgilus*. It shall not, most sage master.
*Tecnicus*. I am jealous;
For if the borrowed shape so late put on
Inferred a consequence, we must conclude
Some violent design of sudden nature
Hath shook that shadow off, to fly upon
A new-hatched execution. Orgilus,

149–51 *Then . . . account* in Q these lines are given to Bassanes
153 *exercise* discipline
3 *jealous* doubtful, suspicious 8 *execution* enterprise

Take heed thou hast not (under our integrity)
Shrouded unlawful plots; our mortal eyes
Pierce not the secrets of your hearts, the gods
Are only privy to them.
  *Orgilus.* Learned Tecnicus,
Such doubts are causeless; and, to clear the truth
From misconceit, the present state commands me.
The Prince of Argos comes himself in person
In quest of great Calantha for his bride,
Our kingdom's heir; besides, mine only sister,
Euphranea, is disposed to Prophilus;
Lastly, the king is sending letters for me
To Athens, for my quick repair to court:
Please to accept these reasons.
  *Tecnicus.* Just ones, Orgilus,
Not to be contradicted: yet beware
Of an unsure foundation; no fair colours
Can fortify a building faintly jointed.
I have observed a growth in thy aspect
Of dangerous extent, sudden, and (look to 't)
I might add, certain—
  *Orgilus.* My aspect? Could art
Run through mine inmost thoughts, it should not sift
An inclination there more than what suited
With justice of mine honour.
  *Tecnicus.* I believe it.
But know then, Orgilus, what honour is:
Honour consists not in a bare opinion
By doing any act that feeds content,
Brave in appearance, 'cause we think it brave;
Such honour comes by accident, not nature,
Proceeding from the vices of our passion,
Which makes our reason drunk. But real honour
Is the reward of virtue, and acquired
By justice, or by valour which for basis
Hath justice to uphold it. He then fails
In honour, who for lucre or revenge
Commits thefts, murthers, treasons, and adulteries,
With such like, by intrenching on just laws,
Whose sovereignty is best preserved by justice.

10–11 (see p. 92)
12 *only* alone
14 *misconceit* misunderstanding
*the . . . me* my actions are governed by the present state of affairs
18 *disposed* betrothed
24 *faintly* weakly
33 *feeds content* satisfies vanity
39 *basis* ed. Bases Q
41 *or* ed. of Q

Thus, as you see how honour must be grounded
On knowledge, not opinion,—for opinion
Relies on probability and accident,
But knowledge on necessity and truth,—
I leave thee to the fit consideration
Of what becomes the grace of real honour,
Wishing success to all thy virtuous meanings.
*Orgilus*. The gods increase thy wisdom, reverend oracle,
And in thy precepts make me ever thrifty.
*Exit* ORGILUS.

*Tecnicus*. I thank thy wish.—Much mystery of fate
Lies hid in that man's fortunes; curiosity
May lead his actions into rare attempts.
But let the gods be moderators still,
No human power can prevent their will.

*Enter* ARMOSTES [*with a casket*]

From whence come 'ee?
*Armostes*. From King Amyclas, (pardon
My interruption of your studies). Here,
In this sealed box, he sends a treasure dear
To him as his crown. 'A prays your gravity,
You would examine, ponder, sift, and bolt
The pith and circumstance of every tittle
The scroll within contains.
*Tecnicus*. What is 't, Armostes?
*Armostes*. It is the health of Sparta, the king's life,
Sinews and safety of the commonwealth;
The sum of what the oracle delivered
When last he visited the prophetic temple
At Delphos: what his reasons are, for which,
After so long a silence, he requires
Your counsel now, grave man, his majesty
Will soon himself acquaint you with.
*Tecnicus*. Apollo
Inspire my intellect.—[*He takes the casket*] The Prince of Argos
Is entertained?
*Armostes*. He is; and has demanded
Our princess for his wife; which I conceive

53 *thrifty* carefully observant
55 *curiosity* undue ingenuity
57 *moderators* adjudicators
58 *prevent* anticipate and forestall
63 *bolt* sieve
70 (see p. 92)
72 *Your* ed. You Q

One special cause the king importunes you
For resolution of the oracle.

*Tecnicus.* My duty to the king, good peace to Sparta,
And fair day to Armostes.

*Armostes.* Like to Tecnicus.

*Exeunt.*

## Act III, Scene ii

*Soft Music. A Song.*

*Can you paint a thought? or number*
*Every fancy in a slumber?*
*Can you count soft minutes roving*
*From a dial's point by moving?*
*Can you grasp a sigh? or, lastly,*
*Rob a virgin's honour chastely?*
*No, oh no! yet you may*
*Sooner do both that and this,*
*This and that, and never miss,*
*Than by any praise display*
*Beauty's beauty; such a glory,*
*As beyond all fate, all story,*
*All arms, all arts,*
*All loves, all hearts,*
*Greater than those, or they,*
*Do, shall, and must obey.*

*During which time enters* PROPHILUS, BASSANES, PENTHEA, GRAUSIS, *passing over the stage.* BASSANES *and* GRAUSIS *enter again softly, stealing to several stands, and listen.*

*Bassanes.* All silent, calm, secure.—Grausis, no creaking?
No noise? Dost hear nothing?

*Grausis.* Not a mouse,
Or whisper of the wind.

*Bassanes.* The floor is matted;
The bed-posts sure are steel or marble.—Soldiers
Should not affect, methinks, strains so effeminate;
Sounds of such delicacy are but fawnings
Upon the sloth of luxury, they heighten
Cinders of covert lust up to a flame.

78 *resolution* interpretation
16 s.d. *several stands* separate positions (see also p. 92)
20–1 (see p. 92) 23 *luxury* lechery

*Grausis.* What do you mean, my lord? Speak low; that
gabbling
Of yours will but undo us.
*Bassanes.* Chamber-combats
Are felt, not heard.
*Prophilus.* [*Within*] 'A wakes.
*Bassanes.* What's that?
*Ithocles.* [*Within*] Who's there?
Sister?—All quit the room else.
*Bassanes.* 'Tis consented.

*Enter* PROPHILUS

*Prophilus.* Lord Bassanes, your brother would be private.
We must forbear; his sleep hath newly left him.
Please 'ee, withdraw.
*Bassanes.* By any means; 'tis fit.
*Prophilus.* Pray, gentlewoman, walk too.
*Grausis* Yes, I will, sir.
*Exeunt omnes.*

ITHOCLES *discovered in a chair, and* PENTHEA

*Ithocles.* Sit nearer, sister, to me; nearer yet.
We had one father, in one womb took life,
Were brought up twins together, yet have lived
At distance, like two strangers. I could wish
That the first pillow whereon I was cradled
Had proved to me a grave.
*Penthea.* You had been happy:
Then had you never known that sin of life,
Which blots all following glories with a vengeance
For forfeiting the last will of the dead,
From whom you had your being.
*Ithocles.* Sad Penthea,
Thou canst not be too cruel; my rash spleen
Hath with a violent hand plucked from thy bosom
A love-blest heart, to grind it into dust;
For which mine's now a-breaking.
*Penthea.* Not yet, heaven,
I do beseech thee. First let some wild fires
Scorch, not consume it. May the heat be cherished
With desires infinite, but hopes impossible.

27 *heard* ed. hard Q 32 (see p. 92)
45 *love-blest* ed. louer-blest Q

*Ithocles.* Wronged soul, thy prayers are heard.
*Penthea.* Here, lo, I breathe,
A miserable creature, led to ruin
By an unnatural brother.
*Ithocles.* I consume
In languishing affections for that trespass;
Yet cannot die.
*Penthea.* The handmaid to the wages
Of country toil drinks the untroubled streams
With leaping kids and with the bleating lambs,
And so allays her thirst secure; whiles I
Quench my hot sighs with fleetings of my tears.
*Ithocles.* The labourer doth eat his coarsest bread,
Earned with his sweat, and lies him down to sleep;
While every bit I touch turns in digestion
To gall, as bitter as Penthea's curse.
Put me to any penance for my tyranny,
And I will call thee merciful.
*Penthea.* Pray kill me;
Rid me from living with a jealous husband;
Then we will join in friendship, be again
Brother and sister.—Kill me, pray: nay, will 'ee?
*Ithocles.* How does thy lord esteem thee?
*Penthea.* Such an one
As only you have made me: a faith-breaker,
A spotted whore. Forgive me; I am one
In act, not in desires, the gods must witness.
*Ithocles.* Thou dost belie thy friend.
*Penthea.* I do not, Ithocles;
For she that's wife to Orgilus, and lives
In known adultery with Bassanes,
Is at the best a whore. Wilt kill me now?
The ashes of our parents will assume
Some dreadful figure, and appear to charge
Thy bloody guilt, that hast betrayed their name
To infamy in this reproachful match.
*Ithocles.* After my victories abroad, at home
I meet despair; ingratitude of nature
Hath made my actions monstrous. Thou shalt stand
A deity, my sister, and be worshipped

54–5 *The . . . toil* the country girl
55 *Of . . . streams* The vntroubled of Country toyle, drinkes streames Q
57 *secure* unmolested
58 *fleetings* streams, flowings
61 *While* ed. Which Q
71 *act* ed. art Q

For thy resolved martyrdom; wronged maids,
And married wives shall to thy hallowed shrine
Offer their orisons, and sacrifice
Pure turtles, crowned with myrtle; if thy pity
Unto a yielding brother's pressure lend
One finger but to ease it.
*Penthea.* Oh, no more.
*Ithocles.* Death waits to waft me to the Stygian banks,
And free me from this chaos of my bondage;
And till thou wilt forgive, I must endure.
*Penthea.* Who is the saint you serve?
*Ithocles.* Friendship, or nearness
Of birth to any but my sister, durst not
Have moved that question. 'Tis a secret, sister,
I dare not murmur to myself.
*Penthea.* Let me,
By your new protestations I conjure 'ee,
Partake her name.
*Ithocles.* Her name,—'tis,—'tis,—I dare not.
*Penthea.* All your respects are forged.
*Ithocles.* They are not.—Peace!
Calantha is the princess, the king's daughter,
Sole heir of Sparta.—Me most miserable!
Do I now love thee? For my injuries
Revenge thyself with bravery, and gossip
My treasons to the king's ears. Do! Calantha
Knows it not yet, nor Prophilus, my nearest.
*Penthea.* Suppose you were contracted to her, would it not
Split even your very soul to see her father
Snatch her out of your arms against her will,
And force her on the Prince of Argos?
*Ithocles.* Trouble not
The fountains of mine eyes with thine own story;
I sweat in blood for't.
*Penthea.* We are reconciled.
Alas, sir, being children, but two branches
Of one stock, 'tis not fit we should divide.
Have comfort, you may find it.
*Ithocles.* Yes, in thee;
Only in thee, Penthea mine.

87 *turtles* turtle doves
93 *nearness* ed. not in Q
95 *'Tis* ed. as Q
99 *All . . . forged* all your fine words to me are lies
103 *bravery* boasting

*Penthea.* If sorrows
Have not too much dulled my infected brain,
I'll cheer invention for an active strain.
*Ithocles.* Mad man! Why have I wronged a maid so excellent?

*Enter* BASSANES *with a poniard,* PROPHILUS, GRONEAS, LEMOPHIL, *and* GRAUSIS

*Bassanes.* I can forbear no longer; more, I will not.
Keep off your hands, or fall upon my point.
Patience is tired; for, like a slow-paced ass,
Ye ride my easy nature, and proclaim
My sloth to vengeance a reproach and property.
*Ithocles.* The meaning of this rudeness?
*Prophilus.* He's distracted.
*Penthea.* Oh, my grieved lord,—
*Grausis.* Sweet lady, come not near him;
He holds his perilous weapon in his hand
To prick 'a cares not whom nor where,—see, see, see!
*Bassanes.* My birth is noble. Though the popular blast
Of vanity, as giddy as thy youth,
Hath reared thy name up to bestride a cloud,
Or progress in the chariot of the sun,
I am no clod of trade, to lackey pride,
Nor, like your slave of expectation, wait
The bawdy hinges of your doors, or whistle
For mystical conveyance to your bed-sports.
*Groneas.* Fine humours! They become him.
*Lemophil.* How 'a stares,
Struts, puffs, and sweats. Most admirable lunacy.
*Ithocles.* But that I may conceive the spirit of wine
Has took possession of your soberer custom,
I'd say you were unmannerly.
*Penthea.* Dear brother,—
*Bassanes.* Unmannerly!—mew, kitling!—smooth formality

117 *cheer . . . strain* try to think what to do
118 s.d. *poniard* dagger
123 *property* personal characteristic
130–1 (see p. 92)
131 *progress* travel ceremoniously
133 *slave of expectation* expectant servant
*wait* attend
135 *mystical* secret
137 *admirable* marvellous
141 *kitling* kitten

Is usher to the rankness of the blood,
But impudence bears up the train. Indeed, sir,
Your fiery mettle, or your springal blaze
Of huge renown, is no sufficient royalty
To print upon my forehead the scorn, 'cuckold'.
*Ithocles.* His jealousy has robbed him of his wits;
'A talks 'a knows not what.
*Bassanes.* Yes, and 'a knows
To whom 'a talks; to one that franks his lust
In swine-security of bestial incest.
*Ithocles.* Ha, devil!
*Bassanes.* I will halloo 't; though I blush more
To name the filthiness than thou to act it.
*Ithocles.* Monster!
*Prophilus.* Sir, by our friendship—
*Penthea.* By our bloods,
Will you quite both undo us, brother?
*Grausis.* Out on him.
These are his megrims, firks, and melancholies.
*Lemophil.* Well said, old touch-hole.
*Groneas.* Kick him out at doors.
*Penthea.* With favour, let me speak.—My lord? what slackness
In my obedience hath deserved this rage?
Except humility and silent duty
Have drawn on your unquiet, my simplicity
Ne'er studied your vexation.
*Bassanes.* Light of beauty,
Deal not ungently with a desperate wound!
No breach of reason dares make war with her
Whose looks are sovereignty, whose breath is balm.
Oh, that I could preserve thee in fruition
As in devotion!
*Penthea.* Sir, may every evil
Locked in Pandora's box shower, in your presence,
On my unhappy head, if, since you made me
A partner in your bed, I have been faulty

144 *springal* youthful 145 *royalty* right
149 *franks* feeds high, crams (see also p. 92)
151 *halloo* proclaim
155 *megrims* fancies, low spirits
*firks* pranks
156 *touch-hole* the hole in the breech of a gun through which the charge is ignited. Used here for 'bawd'
159 *silent* ed. sinlent Q (perhaps for 'sinless')

In one unseemly thought against your honour.
*Ithocles*. Purge not his griefs, Penthea.
*Bassanes*. Yes, say on,
Excellent creature. [*To* ITHOCLES] Good, be not a hindrance
To peace and praise of virtue.—Oh, my senses
Are charmed with sounds celestial.—On, dear, on.
I never gave you one ill word; say, did I?
Indeed I did not.
*Penthea*. Nor, by Juno's forehead,
Was I e'er guilty of a wanton error.
*Bassanes*. A goddess! Let me kneel.
*Grausis*. Alas, kind animal!
*Ithocles*. No; but for penance.
*Bassanes*. Noble sir, what is it?
With gladness I embrace it; yet, pray let not
My rashness teach you to be too unmerciful.
*Ithocles*. When you shall show good proof that manly wisdom,
Not overswayed by passion, or opinion,
Knows how to lead your judgement, then this lady,
Your wife, my sister, shall return in safety
Home, to be guided by you; but, till first
I can out of clear evidence approve it,
She shall be my care.
*Bassanes*. Rip my bosom up,
I'll stand the execution with a constancy:
This torture is unsufferable.
*Ithocles*. Well, sir,
I dare not trust her to your fury.
*Bassanes*. But
Penthea says not so.
*Penthea*. She needs no tongue
To plead excuse, who never purposed wrong.
*Lemophil*. [*To* GRAUSIS] Virgin of reverence and antiquity,
Stay you behind.
*Groneas*. The court wants not your diligence.
*Exeunt omnes, except* BASSANES *and* GRAUSIS.
*Grausis*. What will you do, my lord? My lady's gone;
I am denied to follow.
*Bassanes*. I may see her,
Or speak to her once more?

172 *Good* Good sir
184 *your* ed. not in Q
187 *approve* certify

*Grausis.* And feel her too, man.
Be of good cheer, she's your own flesh and bone.
*Bassanes.* Diseases desperate must find cures alike.
She swore she has been true.
*Grausis.* True, on my modesty.
*Bassanes.* Let him want truth who credits not her vows.
Much wrong I did her, but her brother infinite.
Rumour will voice me the contempt of manhood,
Should I run on thus. Some way I must try
To outdo art, and cry 'a jealousy.
*Exeunt omnes.*

## Act III, Scene iii

*Flourish. Enter* AMYCLAS, NEARCHUS, *leading* CALANTHA, ARMOSTES, CROTOLON, EUPHRANEA, CHRISTALLA, PHILEMA, *and* AMELUS

*Amyclas.* Cousin of Argos, what the heavens have pleased,
In their unchanging counsels, to conclude
For both our kingdoms' weal, we must submit to:
Nor can we be unthankful to their bounties,
Who, when we were even creeping to our grave,
Sent us a daughter, in whose birth our hope
Continues of succession. As you are
In title next, being grandchild to our aunt,
So we in heart desire you may sit nearest
Calantha's love; since we have ever vowed
Not to enforce affection by our will,
But by her own choice to confirm it gladly.
*Nearchus.* You speak the nature of a right just father.
I come not hither roughly to demand
My cousin's thraldom, but to free mine own.
Report of great Calantha's beauty, virtue,
Sweetness, and singular perfections, courted
All ears to credit what I find was published
By constant truth; from which, if any service
Of my desert can purchase fair construction,
This lady must command it.
*Calantha.* Princely sir,
So well you know how to profess observance

200 (see p. 92)
206 To out-doe Art, and cry a Iealousie Q (see also p. 92)
5 *grave* ed. graues Q 22 *observance* courtly service

That you instruct your hearers to become
Practitioners in duty; of which number
I'll study to be chief.

*Nearchus.* Chief, glorious virgin,
In my devotions, as in all men's wonder.

*Amyclas.* Excellent cousin, we deny no liberty;
Use thine own opportunities.—Armostes,
We must consult with the philosophers;
The business is of weight.

*Armostes.* Sir, at your pleasure.

*Amyclas.* You told me, Crotolon, your son's returned
From Athens: wherefore comes 'a not to court
As we commanded?

*Crotolon.* He shall soon attend
Your royal will, great sir.

*Amyclas.* The marriage
Between young Prophilus and Euphranea
Tastes of too much delay.

*Crotolon.* My lord,—

*Amyclas.* Some pleasures
At celebration of it would give life
To th' entertainment of the prince our kinsman.
Our court wears gravity more than we relish.

*Armostes.* Yet the heavens smile on all your high attempts,
Without a cloud.

*Crotolon.* So may the gods protect us.

*Calantha.* A prince a subject?

*Nearchus.* Yes, to beauty's sceptre;
As all hearts kneel, so mine.

*Calantha.* You are too courtly.

*To them* ITHOCLES, ORGILUS, PROPHILUS

*Ithocles.* Your safe return to Sparta is most welcome:
I joy to meet you here, and, as occasion
Shall grant us privacy, will yield you reasons
Why I should covet to deserve the title
Of your respected friend; for, without compliment,
Believe it, Orgilus, 'tis my ambition.

*Orgilus.* Your lordship may command me, your poor servant.

*Ithocles.* [*Aside*] So amorously close?—so soon?—my heart!

27 *cousin* used loosely for any relative
40 *high attempts* noble enterprises
51 *close* ed. close close Q

*Prophilus.* What sudden change is next?
*Ithocles.* Life to the King,
To whom I here present this noble gentleman
New come from Athens. Royal sir, vouchsafe
Your gracious hand in favour of his merit.
*Crotolon.* My son preferred by Ithocles!
*Amyclas.* Our bounties
Shall open to thee, Orgilus; for instance,—
Hark in thine ear—if, out of those inventions
Which flow in Athens, thou hast there ingrossed
Some rarity of wit, to grace the nuptials
Of thy fair sister, and renown our court
In th' eyes of this young prince, we shall be debtor
To thy conceit: think on 't.
*Orgilus.* Your highness honours me.
*Nearchus.* My tongue and heart are twins.
*Calantha.* A noble birth,
Becoming such a father.—Worthy Orgilus,
You are a guest most wished for.
*Orgilus.* May my duty
Still rise in your opinion, sacred princess.
*Ithocles.* Euphranea's brother, sir; a gentleman
Well worthy of your knowledge.
*Nearchus.* We embrace him,
Proud of so dear acquaintance.
*Amyclas.* All prepare
For revels and disport; the joys of Hymen,
Like Phoebus in his lustre, puts to flight
All mists of dullness. Crown the hours with gladness;
No sounds but music, no discourse but mirth.
*Calantha.* Thine arm, I prithee, Ithocles.—Nay, good
My lord, keep on your way, I am provided.
*Nearchus.* I dare not disobey.
*Ithocles.* Most heavenly lady.
*Exeunt.*

56 *preferred* put forward for advancement
59 *flow* abound
*ingrossed* acquired
63 *conceit* idea, invention
67 *Still* Always

## Act III, Scene iv

*Enter* CROTOLON, ORGILUS

*Crotolon.* The king hath spoke his mind.
*Orgilus.* His will he hath;
But were it lawful to hold plea against
The power of greatness, not the reason, haply
Such under-shrubs as subjects sometimes might
Borrow of nature justice, to inform
That licence sovereignty holds without check
Over a meek obedience.
*Crotolon.* How resolve you
Touching your sister's marriage? Prophilus
Is a deserving and a hopeful youth.
*Orgilus.* I envy not his merit, but applaud it;
Could wish him thrift in all his best desires,
And with a willingness inleague our blood
With his, for purchase of full growth in friendship.
He never touched on any wrong that maliced
The honour of our house, nor stirred our peace;
Yet, with your favour, let me not forget
Under whose wing he gathers warmth and comfort,
Whose creature he is bound, made, and must live so.
*Crotolon.* Son, son, I find in thee a harsh condition;
No courtesy can win it; 'tis too rancorous.
*Orgilus.* Good sir, be not severe in your construction;
I am no stranger to such easy calms
As sit in tender bosoms. Lordly Ithocles
Hath graced my entertainment in abundance,
Too humbly hath descended from that height
Of arrogance and spleen which wrought the rape
On grieved Penthea's purity; his scorn
Of my untoward fortunes is reclaimed
Unto a courtship, almost to a fawning:—
I'll kiss his foot, since you will have it so.
*Crotolon.* Since I will have it so? Friend, I will have it so,
Without our ruin by your politic plots,

2 *to hold plea* to try an action at law
5 *inform* shape, control
6 *licence* authority
14 *maliced* threatened
28 *untoward* unprosperous
*reclaimed* changed for the better

5 (see p. 92)
11 *wish* ed. with Q
*thrift* success
19 *condition* state of mind

Or wolf of hatred snarling in your breast.
You have a spirit, sir, have ye? A familiar
That posts i' th' air for your intelligence?
Some such hobgoblin hurried you from Athens,
For yet you come unsent for.

*Orgilus.* If unwelcome,
I might have found a grave there.

*Crotolon.* Sure your business
Was soon dispatched, or your mind altered quickly.

*Orgilus.* 'Twas care, sir, of my health cut short my journey;
For there a general infection
Threatens a desolation.

*Crotolon.* And I fear
Thou hast brought back a worse infection with thee,
Infection of thy mind; which, as thou sayest,
Threatens the desolation of our family.

*Orgilus.* Forbid it, our dear genius! I will rather
Be made a sacrifice on Thrasus' monument,
Or kneel to Ithocles, his son, in dust,
Than woo a father's curse. My sister's marriage
With Prophilus is from my heart confirmed.
May I live hated, may I die despised,
If I omit to further it in all
That can concern me.

*Crotolon.* I have been too rough.
My duty to my king made me so earnest;
Excuse it, Orgilus.

*Orgilus.* Dear sir,—

*Crotolon.* Here comes
Euphranea, with Prophilus and Ithocles.

*Enter to them* PROPHILUS, EUPHRANEA, ITHOCLES, GRONEAS, LEMOPHIL

*Orgilus.* Most honoured!—ever famous!

*Ithocles.* Your true friend,
On earth not any truer.—With smooth eyes
Look on this worthy couple; your consent
Can only make them one.

*Orgilus.* They have it.—Sister,
Thou pawnedst to me an oath, of which engagement
I never will release thee, if thou aimest

35 *posts* journeys
58 *smooth* kindly
46 *genius* guiding spirit
60 *only* alone

At any other choice than this.
*Euphranea.* Dear brother,
At him or none.
*Crotolon.* To which my blessing's added.
*Orgilus.* Which, till a greater ceremony perfect,
Euphranea, lend thy hand. Here take her, Prophilus,
Live long a happy man and wife; and further,
That these in presence may conclude an omen,
Thus for a bridal song I close my wishes:
*Comforts lasting, loves increasing,*
*Like soft hours never ceasing;*
*Plenty's pleasure, peace complying,*
*Without jars, or tongues envying;*
*Hearts by holy union wedded,*
*More than theirs by custom bedded;*
*Fruitful issues; life so graced,*
*Not by age to be defaced;*
*Budding, as the year ensu'th,*
*Every spring another youth:*
*All what thought can add beside,*
*Crown this bridegroom and this bride.*
*Prophilus.* You have sealed joy close to my soul.—
Euphranea,
Now I may call thee mine.
*Ithocles.* I but exchange
One good friend for another.
*Orgilus.* If these gallants
Will please to grace a poor invention
By joining with me in some slight device,
I'll venture on a strain my younger days
Have studied for delight.
*Lemophil.* With thankful willingness
I offer my attendance.
*Groneas.* No endeavour
Of mine shall fail to show itself.
*Ithocles.* We will
All join to wait on thy directions, Orgilus.
*Orgilus.* Oh, my good lord, your favours flow towards
A too unworthy worm; but, as you please,
I am what you will shape me.
*Ithocles.* A fast friend.
*Crotolon.* I thank thee, son, for this acknowledgement;
It is a sight of gladness.
*Orgilus.* But my duty.
*Exeunt omnes.*

## Act III, Scene v

*Enter* CALANTHA, PENTHEA, CHRISTALLA, PHILEMA

*Calantha.* Whoe'er would speak with us, deny his
entrance;
Be careful of our charge.
*Christalla.* We shall, madam.
*Calantha.* Except the king himself, give none admittance;
Not any.
*Philema.* Madam, it shall be our care.
*Exeunt* [CHRISTALLA *and* PHILEMA]
*Calantha.* Being alone, Penthea, you have granted
The opportunity you sought, and might
At all times have commanded.
*Penthea.* 'Tis a benefit
Which I shall owe your goodness even in death for.
My glass of life, sweet princess, hath few minutes
Remaining to run down; the sands are spent;
For by an inward messenger I feel
The summons of departure short and certain.
*Calantha.* You feed too much your melancholy.
*Penthea.* Glories
Of human greatness are but pleasing dreams,
And shadows soon decaying; on the stage
Of my mortality my youth hath acted
Some scenes of vanity, drawn out at length
By varied pleasures, sweetened in the mixture,
But tragical in issue. Beauty, pomp,
With every sensuality our giddiness
Doth frame an idol, are unconstant friends,
When any troubled passion makes assault
On the unguarded castle of the mind.
*Calantha.* Contemn not your condition for the proof
Of bare opinion only: to what end
Reach all these moral texts?
*Penthea.* To place before 'ee
A perfect mirror, wherein you may see

1 *deny* forbid
4 centred below this line Q has 'Calantha, Penthea'
9 *glass* hour-glass 19 *issue* outcome
20 *sensuality* pleasure of the senses
24–5 *for . . . only* just to prove a few general statements

How weary I am of a lingering life,
Who count the best a misery.
*Calantha.* Indeed
You have no little cause; yet none so great
As to distrust a remedy.
*Penthea.* That remedy
Must be a winding-sheet, a fold of lead,
And some untrod-on corner in the earth.
Not to detain your expectation, princess,
I have an humble suit.
*Calantha.* Speak, and enjoy it.
*Penthea.* Vouchsafe, then, to be my executrix,
And take that trouble on 'ee to dispose
Such legacies as I bequeath, impartially.
I have not much to give, the pains are easy;
Heaven will reward your piety, and thank it
When I am dead; for sure I must not live;
I hope I cannot.
*Calantha.* Now, beshrew thy sadness;
Thou turnest me too much woman.
*Penthea.* [*Aside*] Her fair eyes
Melt into passion. Then I have assurance
Encouraging my boldness.—In this paper
My will was charactered; which you, with pardon,
Shall now know from mine own mouth.
*Calantha.* Talk on, prithee:
It is a pretty earnest.
*Penthea.* I have left me
But three poor jewels to bequeath. The first is
My youth; for though I am much old in griefs,
In years I am a child.
*Calantha.* To whom that?
*Penthea.* To virgin-wives, such as abuse not wedlock
By freedom of desires, but covet chiefly
The pledges of chaste beds for ties of love,
Rather than ranging of their blood; and next
To married maids, such as prefer the number
Of honourable issue in their virtues
Before the flattery of delights by marriage:
May those be ever young.
*Calantha.* A second jewel
You mean to part with?

35 *and* ed. I Q
36 speech-prefix not in Q
46 *charactered* written
48 *earnest* foretaste

*Penthea.* 'Tis my fame, I trust
By scandal yet untouched; this I bequeath
To Memory, and Time's old daughter, Truth.
If ever my unhappy name find mention
When I am fallen to dust, may it deserve
Beseeming charity without dishonour.
*Calantha.* How handsomely thou playest with harmless sport
Of mere imagination. Speak the last;
I strangely like thy will.
*Penthea.* This jewel, madam,
Is dearly precious to me; you must use
The best of your discretion to employ
This gift as I intend it.
*Calantha.* Do not doubt me.
*Penthea.* 'Tis long agone since first I lost my heart.
Long have I lived without it, else for certain
I should have given that too; but instead
Of it, to great Calantha, Sparta's heir,
By service bound, and by affection vowed,
I do bequeath, in holiest rites of love,
Mine only brother, Ithocles.
*Calantha.* What saidst thou?
*Penthea.* Impute not, heaven-blest lady, to ambition
A faith as humbly perfect as the prayers
Of a devoted suppliant can endow it.
Look on him, princess, with an eye of pity;
How like the ghost of what he late appeared
'A moves before you.
*Calantha.* Shall I answer here,
Or lend my ear too grossly?
*Penthea.* First his heart
Shall fall in cinders, scorched by your disdain,
Ere he will dare, poor man, to ope an eye
On these divine looks, but with low-bent thoughts
Accusing such presumption. As for words,
'A dares not utter any but of service.
Yet this lost creature loves 'ee.—Be a princess
In sweetness as in blood; give him his doom,
Or raise him up to comfort.
*Calantha.* What new change
Appears in my behaviour, that thou darest

62 (see p. 93) 65 *Beseeming* befitting
85 *grossly* indelicately

Tempt my displeasure?
*Penthea.* I must leave the world
To revel in Elysium, and 'tis just
To wish my brother some advantage here;
Yet, by my best hopes, Ithocles is ignorant
Of this pursuit. But if you please to kill him,
Lend him one angry look, or one harsh word,
And you shall soon conclude how strong a power
Your absolute authority holds over
His life and end.
*Calantha.* You have forgot, Penthea,
How still I have a father.
*Penthea.* But remember
I am a sister, though to me this brother
Hath been, you know, unkind; oh, most unkind.
*Calantha.* Christalla, Philema, where are 'ee?—Lady,
Your check lies in my silence.

*Enter* CHRISTALLA *and* PHILEMA

*Both.* Madam, here.
*Calantha.* I think 'ee sleep, 'ee drones; wait on Penthea
Unto her lodging.—[*Aside*] Ithocles? Wronged lady!
*Penthea.* My reckonings are made even; death or fate
Can now nor strike too soon, nor force too late.
*Exeunt.*

## Act IV, Scene i

*Enter* ITHOCLES *and* ARMOSTES

*Ithocles.* Forbear your inquisition; curiosity
Is of too subtle and too searching nature;
In fears of love too quick, too slow of credit.—
I am not what you doubt me.
*Armostes.* Nephew, be then
As I would wish;—all is not right.—Good heaven
Confirm your resolutions for dependence
On worthy ends, which may advance your quiet.
*Ithocles.* I did the noble Orgilus much injury,
But grieved Penthea more; I now repent it,

96 *in* ed. not in Q    108 *check* rebuke
4 *doubt me* fear me to be
6–7 *resolutions . . . ends* intentions to be honourable

Now, uncle, now; this 'now' is now too late.
So provident is folly in sad issue,
That after-wit, like bankrupts' debts, stands tallied,
Without all possibilities of payment.
Sure he's an honest, very honest gentleman;
A man of single meaning.

*Armostes.* I believe it.
Yet, nephew, 'tis the tongue informs our ears;
Our eyes can never pierce into the thoughts,
For they are lodged too inward:—but I question
No truth in Orgilus.—The princess, sir.

*Ithocles.* The princess? ha!

*Armostes.* With her the prince of Argos.

*Enter* NEARCHUS, *leading* CALANTHA; AMELUS, CHRISTALLA, PHILEMA

*Nearchus.* Great fair one, grace my hopes with any instance
Of livery, from the allowance of your favour.
This little spark—

[*Attempts to take a ring from her finger*]

*Calantha.* A toy!

*Nearchus.* Love feasts on toys,
For Cupid is a child;—vouchsafe this bounty:
It cannot be denied.

*Calantha.* You shall not value,
Sweet cousin, at a price what I count cheap;
So cheap, that let him take it who dares stoop for't,
And give it at next meeting to a mistress.
She'll thank him for 't, perhaps.

[*Casts it to* ITHOCLES]

*Amelus.* The ring, sir, is
The princess's; I could have took it up.

*Ithocles.* Learn manners, prithee.—To the blessed owner,
Upon my knees.

[*Offers it to* CALANTHA]

*Nearchus.* Y' are saucy.

*Calantha.* This is pretty.
I am, belike, 'a mistress'—wondrous pretty.

11 *provident* productive
12 *after-wit* wisdom after the event
*stands* ed. stand Q
13 *Without* Beyond
15 *single* direct, sincere
21–2 *instance of livery* personal article to wear as a sign of service
25 *be denied* ed. beny'd Q

Let the man keep his fortune, since he found it;
He's worthy on 't.—On, cousin.
*Ithocles.* [*To* AMELUS] Follow, spaniel;
I'll force 'ee to a fawning else.
*Amelus.* You dare not.
*Exeunt.* [*Manent* ITHOCLES *and* ARMOSTES]
*Armostes.* My lord, you were too forward.
*Ithocles.* Look 'ee, uncle:
Some such there are whose liberal contents
Swarm without care in every sort of plenty;
Who, after full repasts, can lay them down
To sleep; and they sleep, uncle: in which silence
Their very dreams present 'em choice of pleasures,
Pleasures (observe me, uncle) of rare object:
Here heaps of gold, there increments of honours,
Now change of garments, then the votes of people;
Anon varieties of beauties, courting,
In flatteries of the night, exchange of dalliance;
Yet these are still but dreams. Give me felicity
Of which my senses waking are partakers,
A real, visible, material happiness;
And then, too, when I stagger in expectance
Of the least comfort that can cherish life.—
I saw it, sir, I saw it; for it came
From her own hand.
*Armostes.* The princess threw it t'ee.
*Ithocles.* True, and she said—well I remember what.
Her cousin prince would beg it.
*Armostes.* Yes, and parted
In anger at your taking on 't.
*Ithocles.* Penthea!
Oh, thou hast pleaded with a powerful language!
I want a fee to gratify thy merit;
But I will do—
*Armostes.* What is't you say?
*Ithocles.* In anger!
In anger let him part; for could his breath,
Like whirlwinds, toss such servile slaves as lick
The dust his footsteps print, into a vapour,
It durst not stir a hair of mine. It should not;
I'd rend it up by th' roots first. To be anything
Calantha smiles on, is to be a blessing

38 *liberal contents* easy ways of life
59 *I want . . . merit* I lack means to reward you as you deserve

More sacred than a petty-prince of Argos
Can wish to equal, or in worth or title.
*Armostes.* Contain yourself, my lord. Ixion, aiming
To embrace Juno, bosom'd but a cloud,
And begat Centaurs; 'tis an useful moral.
Ambition hatched in clouds of mere opinion
Proves but in birth a prodigy.
*Ithocles.* I thank 'ee;
Yet, with your licence, I should seem uncharitable
To gentler fate, if, relishing the dainties
Of a soul's settled peace, I were so feeble
Not to digest it.
*Armostes.* He deserves small trust
Who is not privy-counsellor to himself.

*Enter* NEARCHUS, ORGILUS, *and* AMELUS

*Nearchus.* Brave me?
*Orgilus.* Your excellence mistakes his temper;
For Ithocles in fashion of his mind
Is beautiful, soft, gentle, the clear mirror
Of absolute perfection.
*Amelus.* Was 't your modesty
Termed any of the prince his servants 'spaniel'?
Your nurse sure taught you other language.
*Ithocles.* Language?
*Nearchus.* A gallant man-at-arms is here, a doctor
In feats of chivalry, blunt and rough-spoken,
Vouchsafing not the fustian of civility,
Which rash spirits style good manners.
*Ithocles.* Manners?
*Orgilus.* No more, illustrious sir; 'tis matchless Ithocles.
*Nearchus.* You might have understood who I am.
*Ithocles.* Yes,
I did—else—but the presence calmed th' affront;
Y' are cousin to the princess.
*Nearchus.* To the king, too;
A certain instrument that lent supportance
To your colossic greatness—to that king too,
You might have added.
*Ithocles.* There is more divinity
In beauty than in majesty.

69 (see p. 93)
72 *mere opinion* pure fantasy
73 *prodigy* monster
85 *doctor* one qualified to instruct
87 *fustian* bombast
88 (see p. 93)
91 *presence . . . affront* the royal presence prevented violence

*Armostes.* Oh, fie, fie!
*Nearchus.* This odd youth's pride turns heretic in loyalty.
Sirrah! low mushrooms never rival cedars.
*Exeunt* NEARCHUS *and* AMELUS.
*Ithocles.* Come back!—What pitiful dull thing am I
So to be tamely scolded at? Come back!
Let him come back, and echo once again
That scornful sound of 'mushroom'! painted colts—
Like heralds' coats gilt o'er with crowns and sceptres—
May bait a muzzled lion.
*Armostes.* Cousin, cousin,
Thy tongue is not thy friend.
*Orgilus.* In point of honour
Discretion knows no bounds. Amelus told me
'Twas all about a little ring.
*Ithocles.* A ring
The princess threw away, and I took up.
Admit she threw 't to me, what arm of brass
Can snatch it hence? No; could 'a grind the hoop
To powder, 'a might sooner reach my heart
Than steal and wear one dust on't.—Orgilus,
I am extremely wronged.
*Orgilus.* A lady's favour
Is not to be so slighted.
*Ithocles.* Slighted!
*Armostes.* Quiet
These vain unruly passions, which will render ye
Into a madness.
*Orgilus.* Griefs will have their vent.

*Enter* TECNICUS [*with a scroll*]

*Armostes.* Welcome; thou comest in season, reverend man,
To pour the balsam of a suppling patience
Into the festering wound of ill-spent fury.
*Orgilus.* [*Aside*] What makes he here?
*Tecnicus.* The hurts are yet not mortal,
Which shortly will prove deadly. To the king,
Armostes, see in safety thou deliver
This sealed-up counsel; bid him with a constancy
Peruse the secrets of the gods.—Oh, Sparta,

102–4 (see p. 93)
112 *dust* particle
118 *suppling* ed. supplying Q
120–1 (see p. 93)

Oh, Lacedemon! double named, but one
In fate: when kingdoms reel (mark well my saw)
Their heads must needs be giddy. Tell the king
That henceforth he no more must enquire after
My aged head: Apollo wills it so.
I am for Delphos.

*Armostes.* Not without some conference
With our great master?

*Tecnicus.* Never more to see him:
A greater prince commands me.—Ithocles,
*When youth is ripe, and age from time doth part,*
*The lifeless trunk shall wed the broken heart.*

*Ithocles.* What's this, if understood?

*Tecnicus.* List, Orgilus;
Remember what I told thee long before.
These tears shall be my witness.

*Armostes.* 'Las, good man.

*Tecnicus.* Let craft with courtesy a while confer,
Revenge proves its own executioner.

*Orgilus.* Dark sentences are for Apollo's priests;
I am not Œdipus.

*Tecnicus.* My hour is come.
Cheer up the king; farewell to all.—Oh, Sparta,
Oh, Lacedemon!

*Exit* TECNICUS

*Armostes.* If prophetic fire
Have warmed this old man's bosom, we might construe
His words to fatal sense.

*Ithocles.* Leave to the powers
Above us the effects of their decrees;
My burthen lies within me. Servile fears
Prevent no great effects.—Divine Calantha!

*Armostes.* The gods be still propitious.

*Exeunt* [ITHOCLES *and* ARMOSTES]

*Manet* ORGILUS

*Orgilus.* Something oddly
The book-man prated; yet 'a talked it weeping:
*Let craft with courtesy a while confer,*
*Revenge proves its own executioner.*
Con it again;—for what? It shall not puzzle me;
'Tis dotage of a withered brain.—Penthea

126 *saw* proverbial saying 138 (see p. 93)
141 *Œdipus* who solved the riddle of the Sphinx
148 *Prevent* go before

Forbade me not her presence; I may see her,
And gaze my fill. Why see her then I may,
When, if I faint to speak, I must be silent.

*Exit* ORGILUS.

## Act IV, Scene ii

*Enter* BASSANES, GRAUSIS, *and* PHULAS

*Bassanes*. Pray, use your recreations. All the service
I will expect is quietness amongst 'ee.
Take liberty at home, abroad, at all times,
And in your charities appease the gods
Whom I, with my distractions, have offended.
*Grausis*. Fair blessings on thy heart.
*Phulas*. Here's a rare change!
My lord, to cure the itch, is surely gelded;
The cuckold in conceit hath cast his horns.
*Bassanes*. Betake 'ee to your several occasions;
And wherein I have heretofore been faulty,
Let your constructions mildly pass it over.
Henceforth I'll study reformation,—more
I have not for employment.
*Grausis*. Oh, sweet man!
Thou art the very 'Honeycomb of Honesty'.
*Phulas*. The 'Garland of Good-will'.—Old lady, hold up
Thy reverend snout, and trot behind me softly,
As it becomes a moil of ancient carriage.

*Exeunt. Manet* BASSANES.

*Bassanes*. Beasts, only capable of sense, enjoy
The benefit of food and ease with thankfulness;
Such silly creatures, with a grudging, kick not
Against the portion nature hath bestowed:
But men, endowed with reason, and the use
Of reason, to distinguish from the chaff
Of abject scarcity the quintessence,
Soul, and elixir of the earth's abundance,
The treasures of the sea, the air, nay, heaven,
Repining at these glories of creation

8 *in conceit* in imagination 14–15 (see p. 93)
17 *moil* mule
18 *capable of sense* able to receive only sense-impressions (see also p. 93) 24–5 (see p. 93)

Are verier beasts than beasts; and of those beasts
The worst am I. I, who was made a monarch
Of what a heart could wish for, a chaste wife,
Endeavoured what in me lay to pull down
That temple built for adoration only,
And level 't in the dust of causeless scandal.
But, to redeem a sacrilege so impious,
Humility shall pour, before the deities
I have incensed, a largess of more patience
Than their displeased altars can require.
No tempests of commotion shall disquiet
The calms of my composure.

*Enter* ORGILUS

*Orgilus.* I have found thee,
Thou patron of more horrors than the bulk
Of manhood, hooped about with ribs of iron,
Can cram within thy breast. Penthea, Bassanes,
Cursed by thy jealousies,—more, by thy dotage,—
Is left a prey to words.
*Bassanes.* Exercise
Your trials for addition to my penance;
I am resolved.
*Orgilus.* Play not with misery
Past cure. Some angry minister of fate hath
Deposed the empress of her soul, her reason,
From its most proper throne; but,—what's the miracle
More new,—I, I have seen it, and yet live.
*Bassanes.* You may delude my senses, not my judgement;
'Tis anchored into a firm resolution;
Dalliance of mirth or wit can ne'er unfix it.
Practise yet further.
*Orgilus.* May thy death of love to her
Damn all thy comforts to a lasting fast
From every joy of life. Thou barren rock,
By thee we have been split in ken of harbour.

*Enter* ITHOCLES, PENTHEA, *her hair about her ears*, [ARMOSTES], PHILEMA, CHRISTALLA

*Ithocles.* Sister, look up; your Ithocles, your brother
Speaks t'ee; why do you weep? Dear, turn not from me.—
Here is a killing sight; lo, Bassanes,

36 *largess* ed. largenesse Q
54 *Practise yet further* Go on, say what you like
57 *ken* sight

A lamentable object.
*Orgilus.* Man, dost see it?
Sports are more gamesome; am I yet in merriment?
Why dost not laugh?
*Bassanes.* Divine and best of ladies,
Please to forget my outrage; mercy ever
Cannot but lodge under a roof so excellent.
I have cast off that cruelty of frenzy
Which once appeared, impostor, and then juggled
To cheat my sleeps of rest.
*Orgilus.* Was I in earnest?
*Penthea.* Sure, if we were all Sirens, we should sing pitifully;
And 'twere a comely music, when in parts
One sung another's knell. The turtle sighs
When he hath lost his mate; and yet some say
'A must be dead first. 'Tis a fine deceit
To pass away in a dream; indeed, I've slept
With mine eyes open a great while. No falsehood
Equals a broken faith; there's not a hair
Sticks on my head but like a leaden plummet
It sinks me to the grave. I must creep thither;
The journey is not long.
*Ithocles.* But thou, Penthea,
Hast many years, I hope, to number yet,
Ere thou canst travel that way.
*Bassanes.* Let the sun first
Be wrapped up in an everlasting darkness,
Before the light of nature, chiefly formed
For the whole world's delight, feel an eclipse
So universal.
*Orgilus.* Wisdom, look 'ee, begins
To rave.—Art thou mad, too, antiquity?
*Penthea.* Since I was first a wife I might have been
Mother to many pretty prattling babes.
They would have smiled when I smiled, and for certain
I should have cried when they cried:—truly, brother,
My father would have picked me out a husband,
And then my little ones had been no bastards.
But 'tis too late for me to marry now,
I am past child-bearing; 'tis not my fault.

65 *roof* ed. root Q 67 *impostor* ed. (Impostors Q) a deceiving spirit
71 *turtle* dove 81 *sun* ed. Swan Q

*Bassanes.* Fall on me, if there be a burning Etna,
And bury me in flames. Sweats hot as sulphur
Boil through my pores. Affliction hath in store
No torture like to this.
*Orgilus.* Behold a patience!
Lay by thy whining grey dissimulation,
Do something worth a chronicle; show justice
Upon the author of this mischief; dig out
The jealousies that hatched this thraldom first
With thine own poniard. Every antic rapture
Can roar as thine does.
*Ithocles.* Orgilus, forbear.
*Bassanes.* Disturb him not; it is a talking motion
Provided for my torment. What a fool am I
To bawdy passion! Ere I'll speak a word,
I will look on and burst.
*Penthea.* [*To* ORGILUS] I loved you once.
*Orgilus.* Thou didst, wronged creature, in despite of malice;
For it I love thee ever.
*Penthea.* Spare your hand;
Believe me, I'll not hurt it.
*Orgilus.* Pain my heart too!
*Penthea.* Complain not though I wring it hard. I'll kiss it;
Oh, 'tis a fine soft palm! hark, in thine ear:
Like whom do I look, prithee? Nay, no whispering.
Goodness! we had been happy; too much happiness
Will make folk proud, they say—but that is he—
*Points at* ITHOCLES
And yet he paid for 't home; alas, his heart
Is crept into the cabinet of the princess;
We shall have points and bride-laces. Remember,
When we last gathered roses in the garden,
I found my wits; but truly you lost yours.
That's he, and still 'tis he.
[*Points at* ITHOCLES *again*]
*Ithocles.* Poor soul, how idly
Her fancies guide her tongue.

103 *antic rapture* stage passion
105 *motion* puppet
110 *Spare* Give me
111 *too* ed. to Q
112 speech-prefix not in Q
112 (see p. 94)
119 *points and bride-laces* souvenirs of a wedding
120 (see p. 94)
122 *idly* madly

*Bassanes.* Keep in, vexation,
And break not into clamour.
*Orgilus.* She has tutored me;
Some powerful inspiration checks my laziness.—
Now let me kiss your hand, grieved beauty.
*Penthea.* Kiss it.—
Alack, alack, his lips be wondrous cold;
Dear soul, h'as lost his colour: have 'ee seen
A straying heart? All crannies! every drop
Of blood is turned to an amethyst,
Which married bachelors hang in their ears.
*Orgilus.* Peace usher her into Elysium.
If this be madness, madness is an oracle.
*Exit* ORGILUS.
*Ithocles.* Christalla, Philema, when slept my sister?
Her ravings are so wild.
*Christalla.* Sir, not these ten days.
*Philema.* We watch by her continually; besides,
We cannot any way pray her to eat.
*Bassanes.* Oh,—misery of miseries!
*Penthea.* Take comfort;
You may live well, and die a good old man.
By yea and nay, an oath not to be broken,
If you had joined our hands once in the temple,—
'Twas since my father died, for had he lived
He would have done 't,—I must have called you father.
Oh, my wracked honour, ruined by those tyrants,
A cruel brother and a desperate dotage!
There is no peace left for a ravished wife,
Widowed by lawless marriage; to all memory
Penthea's, poor Penthea's name is strumpeted:
But since her blood was seasoned by the forfeit
Of noble shame with mixtures of pollution,
Her blood—'tis just—be henceforth never heightened
With taste of sustenance. Starve; let that fullness
Whose pleurisy hath fevered faith and modesty—
Forgive me; oh, I faint!
*Armostes.* Be not so wilful,
Sweet niece, to work thine own destruction.
*Ithocles.* Nature
Will call her daughter monster.—What? Not eat?
Refuse the only ordinary means

125 *checks my laziness* reproaches my delay
130 (see p. 94)
140 (see p. 94)
153 *pleurisy* excess

Which are ordained for life? Be not, my sister,
A murtheress to thyself.—Hearest thou this, Bassanes?
*Bassanes*. Foh! I am busy; for I have not thoughts
Enough to think: all shall be well anon.
'Tis tumbling in my head; there is a mastery
In art to fatten and keep smooth the outside;
Yes, and to comfort up the vital spirits
Without the help of food; fumes or perfumes,
Perfumes or fumes. Let her alone; I'll search out
The trick on 't.
*Penthea*. Lead me gently; heavens reward ye.
Griefs are sure friends; they leave, without control,
Nor cure nor comforts for a leprous soul.

*Exeunt the maids supporting* PENTHEA

*Bassanes*. I grant t'ee; and will put in practice instantly
What you shall still admire: 'tis wonderful,
'Tis super-singular, not to be matched;
Yet when I've done't, I've done't:—ye shall all thank me.

*Exit* BASSANES.

*Armostes*. The sight is full of terror.
*Ithocles*. On my soul
Lies such an infinite clog of massy dulness,
As that I have not sense enough to feel it.—
See, uncle, th' angry thing returns again;
Shall's welcome him with thunder? We are haunted,
And must use exorcism to conjure down
This spirit of malevolence.
*Armostes*. Mildly, nephew.

*Enter* NEARCHUS *and* AMELUS

*Nearchus*. I come not, sir, to chide your late disorder,
Admitting that th' inurement to a roughness
In soldiers of your years and fortunes, chiefly,
So lately prosperous, hath not yet shook off
The custom of the war in hours of leisure;
Nor shall you need excuse, since y' are to render
Account to that fair excellence, the princess,
Who in her private gallery expects it
From your own mouth alone: I am a messenger
But to her pleasure.
*Ithocles*. Excellent Nearchus,
Be prince still of my services, and conquer

162 (see p. 94) 171 *admire* wonder at
177 *angry* ed. augury Q 191 *still* ever

Without the combat of dispute; I honour 'ee.
*Nearchus.* The king is on a sudden indisposed,
Physicians are called for; 'twere fit, Armostes,
You should be near him.
*Armostes.* Sir, I kiss your hands.

*Exeunt. Manent* NEARCHUS & AMELUS.

*Nearchus.* Amelus, I perceive Calantha's bosom
Is warmed with other fires than such as can
Take strength from any fuel of the love
I might address to her. Young Ithocles,
Or ever I mistake, is lord ascendant
Of her devotions; one, to speak him truly,
In every disposition nobly fashioned.
*Amelus.* But can your highness brook to be so rivalled,
Considering th' inequality of the persons?
*Nearchus.* I can, Amelus; for affections injured
By tyranny or rigour of compulsion,
Like tempest-threatened trees unfirmly rooted,
Ne'er spring to timely growth: observe, for instance,
Life-spent Penthea, and unhappy Orgilus.
*Amelus.* How does your grace determine?
*Nearchus.* To be jealous
In public of what privately I'll further;
And though they shall not know, yet they shall find it.

*Exeunt omnes.*

## Act IV, Scene iii

*Enter* LEMOPHIL *and* GRONEAS *leading* AMYCLAS, *and placing him in a chair; followed by* ARMOSTES [*with a box*], CROTOLON *and* PROPHILUS

*Amyclas.* Our daughter is not near?
*Armostes.* She is retired, sir,
Into her gallery.
*Amyclas.* Where's the prince our cousin?
*Prophilus.* New walked into the grove, my lord.
*Amyclas.* All leave us
Except Armostes, and you, Crotolon;
We would be private.

200 (see p. 94)

*Prophilus.* Health unto your Majesty.
*Exeunt* PROPHILUS, LEMOPHIL & GRONEAS.
*Amyclas.* What! Tecnicus is gone?
*Armostes.* He is to Delphos;
And to your royal hands presents this box.
*Amyclas.* Unseal it, good Armostes; therein lies
The secrets of the oracle; out with it:
Apollo live our patron. Read, Armostes.
*Armostes.* *The plot in which the vine takes root*
*Begins to dry from head to foot;*
*The stock soon withering, want of sap*
*Doth cause to quail the budding grape;*
*But from the neighbouring elm a dew*
*Shall drop, and feed the plot anew.*
*Amyclas.* That is the oracle; what exposition
Makes the philosopher?
*Armostes.* This brief one only.
*The plot is Sparta, the dried vine the king,*
*The quailing grape his daughter; but the thing*
*Of most importance, not to be revealed,*
*Is a near prince, the elm: the rest concealed.*
*Tecnicus.*
*Amyclas.* Enough; although the opening of this riddle
Be but itself a riddle, yet we construe
How near our labouring age draws to a rest.
But must Calantha quail too—that young grape
Untimely budded? I could mourn for her;
Her tenderness hath yet deserved no rigour
So to be crossed by fate.
*Armostes.* You misapply, sir,—
With favour let me speak it,—what Apollo
Hath clouded in hid sense. I here conjecture
Her marriage with some neighbouring prince, the dew
Of which befriending elm shall ever strengthen
Your subjects with a sovereignty of power.
*Crotolon.* Besides, most gracious lord, the pith of oracles
Is to be then digested when th' events
Expound their truth, not brought as soon to light
As uttered. Truth is child of Time; and herein
I find no scruple, rather cause of comfort,

14 *quail* dry up, die (deliberately ambiguous)
24 *opening* interpretation
39 (see p. 94)
40 *scruple* small, troubling point

With unity of kingdoms.
*Amyclas.* May it prove so,
For weal of this dear nation.—Where is Ithocles?—
Armostes, Crotolon, when this withered vine
Of my frail carcass, on the funeral pile
Is fired into its ashes, let that young man
Be hedged about still with your cares and loves.
Much owe I to his worth, much to his service.—
Let such as wait come in now.
*Armostes.* All attend here.

*Enter* ITHOCLES, CALANTHA, PROPHILUS, ORGILUS, EUPHRANEA, LEMOPHIL, *and* GRONEAS

*Calantha.* Dear sir, king, father!
*Ithocles.* Oh, my royal master!
*Amyclas.* Cleave not my heart (sweet twins of my life's solace)
With your forejudging fears: there is no physic
So cunningly restorative to cherish
The fall of age, or call back youth and vigour,
As your consents in duty. I will shake off
This languishing disease of time, to quicken
Fresh pleasures in these drooping hours of sadness.
Is fair Euphranea married yet to Prophilus?
*Crotolon.* This morning, gracious lord.
*Orgilus.* This very morning;
Which, with your highness' leave, you may observe too.
Our sister looks, methinks, mirthful and sprightly,
As if her chaster fancy could already
Expound the riddle of her gain in losing
A trifle maids know only that they know not.
Pish! prithee, blush not; 'tis but honest change
Of fashion in the garment, loose for straight,
And so the modest maid is made a wife.
Shrewd business—is't not, sister?
*Euphranea.* You are pleasant.
*Amyclas.* We thank thee, Orgilus; this mirth becomes thee.
But wherefore sits the court in such a silence?
A wedding without revels is not seemly.
*Calantha.* Your late indisposition, sir, forbade it.
*Amyclas.* Be it thy charge, Calantha, to set forward
The bridal sports, to which I will be present;

69 (see p. 94)

If not, at least consenting.—Mine own Ithocles,
I have done little for thee yet.
*Ithocles.* Y' have built me
To the full height I stand in.
*Calantha.* [*Aside*] Now or never.—
May I propose a suit?
*Amyclas.* Demand, and have it.
*Calantha.* Pray, sir, give me this young man, and no further
Account him yours than he deserves in all things
To be thought worthy mine. I will esteem him
According to his merit.
*Amyclas.* Still th' art my daughter,
Still growest upon my heart.—[*To* ITHOCLES] Give me thine hand.—
Calantha, take thine own; in noble actions
Thou'lt find him firm and absolute.—I would not
Have parted with thee, Ithocles, to any
But to a mistress who is all what I am.
*Ithocles.* A change, great king, most wished for, 'cause the same.
*Calantha.* Th' art mine.—Have I now kept my word?
*Ithocles.* Divinely.
*Orgilus.* Rich fortunes, guard to favour of a princess,
Rock thee, brave man, in ever-crowned plenty.
Y' are minion of the time; be thankful for it.—
[*Aside*] Ho! here's a swinge in destiny. Apparent,
The youth is up on tiptoe, yet may stumble.
*Amyclas.* On to your recreations.—Now convey me
Unto my bed-chamber; none on his forehead
Wear a distempered look.
*All.* The gods preserve 'ee.
*Calantha.* Sweet, be not from my sight.
*Ithocles.* My whole felicity.

*Exeunt, carrying out of the king.* ORGILUS *stays* ITHOCLES.

*Orgilus.* Shall I be bold, my lord?
*Ithocles.* Thou canst not, Orgilus.
Call me thine own; for Prophilus must henceforth
Be all thy sister's. Friendship, though it cease not
In marriage, yet is oft at less command
Than when a single freedom can dispose it.

84 *absolute* perfect
88 (see p. 94)
89 *fortunes*, ed. fortuness Q
91 *minion of the time* favourite of the hour
92 *Apparent* Obviously
96 *Wear* ed. Were Q

*Orgilus.* Most right, my most good lord, my most great lord,
My gracious princely lord,—I might add, royal.
*Ithocles.* Royal? A subject royal?
*Orgilus.* Why not, pray, sir?
The sovereignty of kingdoms, in their nonage,
Stooped to desert, not birth; there's as much merit
In clearness of affection as in puddle
Of generation. You have conquered love
Even in the loveliest; if I greatly err not,
The son of Venus hath bequeathed his quiver
To Ithocles his manage, by whose arrows
Calantha's breast is opened.
*Ithocles.* Can 't be possible?
*Orgilus.* I was myself a piece of suitor once,
And forward in preferment, too; so forward
That, speaking truth, I may without offence, sir,
Presume to whisper that my hopes, and (hark 'ee)
My certainty of marriage stood assured
With as firm footing (by your leave) as any's
Now at this very instant—but—
*Ithocles.* 'Tis granted:
And for a league of privacy between us,
Read o'er my bosom and partake a secret:
The princess is contracted mine.
*Orgilus.* Still, why not?
I now applaud her wisdom. When your kingdom
Stands seated in your will, secure and settled,
I dare pronounce you will be a just monarch:
Greece must admire and tremble.
*Ithocles.* Then the sweetness
Of so imparadised a comfort, Orgilus!
It is to banquet with the gods.
*Orgilus.* The glory
Of numerous children, potency of nobles,
Bent knees, hearts paved to tread on!
*Ithocles.* With a friendship
So dear, so fast as thine.
*Orgilus.* I am unfitting
For office; but for service—

108 *clearness of affection* nobility of character
108–9 *puddle Of generation* dark workings of heredity
112 *manage* management
123 *Still* Even so

*Ithocles.* We'll distinguish
Our fortunes merely in the title; partners
In all respects else but the bed.
*Orgilus.* The bed?
Forfend it Jove's own jealousy!—till lastly
We slip down in the common earth together.
And there our beds are equal, save some monument
To show this was the king, and this the subject.
*Soft sad music*
List, what sad sounds are these?—extremely sad ones.
*Ithocles.* Sure from Penthea's lodgings.
*Orgilus.* Hark! a voice too.

*A Song* [*within*]

*Oh, no more, no more, too late*
*Sighs are spent; the burning tapers*
*Of a life as chaste as fate,*
*Pure as are unwritten papers,*
*Are burnt out: no heat, no light*
*Now remains; 'tis ever night.*
*Love is dead; let lovers' eyes,*
*Locked in endless dreams,*
*Th' extremes of all extremes,*
*Ope no more, for now Love dies,*
*Now Love dies,—implying*
*Love's martyrs must be ever, ever dying.*

*Ithocles.* Oh, my misgiving heart!
*Orgilus.* A horrid stillness
Succeeds this deathful air; let's know the reason.
Tread softly; there is mystery in mourning.
*Exeunt.*

## Act IV, Scene iv

*Enter* CHRISTALLA *and* PHILEMA, *bringing in* PENTHEA *in a chair, veiled: two other servants placing two chairs, one on the one side, and the other with an engine on the other. The Maids sit down at her feet, mourning. The servants go out: meet them* ITHOCLES *and* ORGILUS.

*Servant.* [*Aside to* ORGILUS] 'Tis done; that on her right hand.

139 s.d. follows 141 in Q
s.d. *engine* mechanism (see also p. 94)

*Orgilus.* Good: begone.

[*Exeunt* SERVANTS]

*Ithocles.* Soft peace enrich this room.

*Orgilus.* How fares the lady?

*Philema.* Dead.

*Christalla.* Dead!

*Philema.* Starved.

*Christalla.* Starved!

*Ithocles.* Me miserable!

*Orgilus.* Tell us,
How parted she from life?

*Philema.* She called for music,
And begged some gentle voice to tune a farewell
To life and griefs. Christalla touched the lute;
I wept the funeral song.

*Christalla.* Which scarce was ended,
But her last breath sealed up these hollow sounds:
'Oh, cruel Ithocles, and injured Orgilus!'
So down she drew her veil, so died.

*Ithocles.* So died.

*Orgilus.* Up! you are messengers of death; go from us.
Here's woe enough to court without a prompter.
Away; and hark ye,—till you see us next,
No syllable that she is dead.—Away.
Keep a smooth brow.

*Exeunt* PHILEMA & CHRISTALLA.

My lord,—

*Ithocles.* Mine only sister!
Another is not left me.

*Orgilus.* Take that chair;
I'll seat me here in this. Between us sits
The object of our sorrows. Some few tears
We'll part among us; I perhaps can mix
One lamentable story to prepare 'em.
There, there; sit there, my lord.

*Ithocles.* Yes, as you please.

ITHOCLES *sits down, and is catch'd in the engine.*

What means this treachery?

*Orgilus.* Caught! you are caught,
Young master. 'Tis thy throne of coronation,
Thou fool of greatness. See, I take this veil off:
Survey a beauty withered by the flames
Of an insulting Phaeton, her brother.

26 *insulting* arrogant
(see also p. 95)

*Ithocles*. Thou meanest to kill me basely?
*Orgilus*. I foreknew
The last act of her life, and trained thee hither
To sacrifice a tyrant to a turtle.
You dreamt of kingdoms, did 'ee? How to bosom
The delicacies of a youngling princess;
How with this nod to grace that subtle courtier,
How with that frown to make this noble tremble,
And so forth; whiles Penthea's groans and tortures,
Her agonies, her miseries, afflictions,
Ne'er touched upon your thought. As for my injuries,
Alas, they were beneath your royal pity;
But yet they lived, thou proud man, to confound thee.
Behold thy fate, this steel. [*Draws a dagger*]
*Ithocles*. Strike home. A courage
As keen as thy revenge shall give it welcome.
But prithee, faint not; if the wound close up,
Tent it with double force, and search it deeply.
Thou lookest that I should whine and beg compassion,
As loath to leave the vainness of my glories;
A statelier resolution arms my confidence,
To cozen thee of honour. Neither could I,
With equal trial of unequal fortune,
By hazard of a duel; 'twere a bravery
Too mighty for a slave intending murther.
On to the execution, and inherit
A conflict with thy horrors.
*Orgilus*. By Apollo,
Thou talkst a goodly language! for requital
I will report thee to thy mistress richly.
And take this peace along: some few short minutes
Determined, my resolves shall quickly follow
Thy wrathful ghost; then, if we tug for mastery,
Penthea's sacred eyes shall lend new courage.
Give me thy hand. Be healthful in thy parting
From lost mortality. Thus, thus, I free it.
[*Stabs him*]
*Ithocles*. Yet, yet, I scorn to shrink.
*Orgilus*. Keep up thy spirit:
I will be gentle even in blood; to linger

28 *trained* lured
42 *Tent* probe (see also p. 95)
46 *cozen* cheat
48 *bravery* distinction
55 *Determined* concluded
59 *Stabs him* ed. kils him Q

Pain, which I strive to cure, were to be cruel.
[*Stabs him again*]

*Ithocles*. Nimble in vengeance, I forgive thee. Follow
Safety, with best success; oh, may it prosper!
Penthea, by thy side thy brother bleeds;
The earnest of his wrongs to thy forced faith.
Thoughts of ambition, or delicious banquet,
With beauty, youth, and love, together perish
In my last breath, which on the sacred altar
Of a long-looked-for peace—now—moves—to heaven.
[*Dies*]

*Orgilus*. Farewell, fair spring of manhood. Henceforth welcome
Best expectation of a noble sufferance.
I'll lock the bodies safe, till what must follow
Shall be approved.—Sweet twins, shine stars for ever.
In vain they build their hopes whose life is shame:
No monument lasts but a happy name.
*Exit* ORGILUS.

## Act V, Scene i

*Enter* BASSANES, *alone*

*Bassanes*. Athens—to Athens I have sent, the nursery
Of Greece for learning, and the fount of knowledge;
For here in Sparta there's not left amongst us
One wise man to direct; we're all turned madcaps.
'Tis said Apollo is the god of herbs,
Then certainly he knows the virtue of 'em:
To Delphos I have sent too. If there can be
A help for nature, we are sure yet.

*Enter* ORGILUS

*Orgilus*. Honour
Attend thy counsels ever.
*Bassanes*. I beseech thee
With all my heart, let me go from thee quietly;
I will not aught to do with thee, of all men.
The doubles of a hare, or, in a morning,

66 *earnest* payment
7 *too* ed. to Q
74 *approved* tested by experience
12 *doubles* ed. doublers Q (see also p. 95)

Salutes from a splay-footed witch, to drop
Three drops of blood at th' nose just, and no more,
Croaking of ravens, or the screech of owls,
Are not so boding mischief as thy crossing
My private meditations. Shun me, prithee;
And if I cannot love thee heartily,
I'll love thee as well as I can.

*Orgilus.* Noble Bassanes,
Mistake me not.

*Bassanes.* Phew! then we shall be troubled.
Thou wert ordained my plague—heaven make me thankful,—
And give me patience too, heaven, I beseech thee.

*Orgilus.* Accept a league of amity; for henceforth,
I vow, by my best genius, in a syllable,
Never to speak vexation. I will study
Service and friendship, with a zealous sorrow
For my past incivility towards 'ee.

*Bassanes.* Heyday! good words, good words. I must believe 'em,
And be a coxcomb for my labour.

*Orgilus.* Use not
So hard a language; your misdoubt is causeless.
For instance, if you promise to put on
A constancy of patience, such a patience
As chronicle or history ne'er mentioned,
As follows not example, but shall stand
A wonder, and a theme for imitation,
The first, the index pointing to a second,
I will acquaint 'ee with an unmatched secret,
Whose knowledge to your griefs shall set a period.

*Bassanes.* Thou canst not, Orgilus; 'tis in the power
Of the gods only. Yet, for satisfaction,
Because I note an earnest in thine utterance,
Unforced and naturally free, be resolute
The virgin-bays shall not withstand the lightning
With a more careless danger than my constancy
The full of thy relation. Could it move
Distraction in a senseless marble statue,
It should find me a rock. I do expect now

13–14 (see p. 95). 24 *genius* guiding spirit
34 *follows not example* has no precedent
36 *index* Printer's pointing hand
42 *resolute* assured 43 (see p. 95)
44 *more careless* greater contempt of

Some truth of unheard moment.
*Orgilus.* To your patience
You must add privacy, as strong in silence
As mysteries locked up in Jove's own bosom.
*Bassanes.* A skull hid in the earth a treble age
Shall sooner prate.
*Orgilus.* Lastly, to such direction
As the severity of a glorious action
Deserves to lead your wisdom and your judgement,
You ought to yield obedience.
*Bassanes.* With assurance
Of will and thankfulness.
*Orgilus.* With manly courage
Please then to follow me.
*Bassanes.* Where'er, I fear not.
*Exeunt omnes.*

## Act V, Scene ii

*Loud music. Enter* GRONEAS *and* LEMOPHIL, *leading* EUPHRANEA; CHRISTALLA *and* PHILEMA, *leading* PROPHILUS; NEARCHUS *supporting* CALANTHA; CROTOLON *and* AMELUS. *Cease loud music; all make a stand.*

*Calantha.* We miss our servant Ithocles, and Orgilus;
On whom attend they?
*Crotolon.* My son, gracious princess,
Whispered some new device, to which these revels
Should be but usher: wherein I conceive
Lord Ithocles and he himself are actors.
*Calantha.* A fair excuse for absence: as for Bassanes,
Delights to him are troublesome. Armostes
Is with the king?
*Crotolon.* He is.
*Calantha.* On to the dance.—
Dear cousin, hand you the bride; the bridegroom must be
Intrusted to my courtship. Be not jealous,
Euphranea; I shall scarcely prove a temptress.—
Fall to our dance.

48 *unheard moment* unprecedented importance
3 *device* performance

*Music.* NEARCHUS *dance with* EUPHRANEA, PROPHILUS *with* CALANTHA, CHRISTALLA *with* LEMOPHIL, PHILEMA *with* GRONEAS. *Dance the first change; during which Enter* ARMOSTES

*Armostes.* (*In* CALANTHA'S *ear*) The king your father's dead.
*Calantha.* To the other change.
*Armostes.* Is 't possible?

*Dance again.*

*Enter* BASSANES

*Bassanes.* Oh, madam!
Penthea, poor Penthea's starved.
*Calantha.* Beshrew thee;
Lead to the next.
*Bassanes.* Amazement dulls my senses.

*Dance again.*

*Enter* ORGILUS

*Orgilus.* Brave Ithocles is murthered, murthered cruelly.
*Calantha.* How dull this music sounds! Strike up more sprightly;
Our footings are not active like our heart,
Which treads the nimbler measure.
*Orgilus.* I am thunderstruck.

*Last change. Cease music.*

*Calantha.* So! let us breathe a while.—Hath not this motion
Raised fresher colour on your cheeks?
*Nearchus.* Sweet princess,
A perfect purity of blood enamels
The beauty of your white.
*Calantha.* We all look cheerfully;
And, cousin, 'tis, methinks, a rare presumption
In any who prefer our lawful pleasures
Before their own sour censure, to interrupt
The custom of this ceremony bluntly.
*Nearchus.* None dares, lady.
*Calantha.* Yes, yes; some hollow voice delivered to me
How that the king was dead.
*Armostes.* The king is dead.
That fatal news was mine; for in mine arms

12 s. d. *change* figure of the dance
25 *prefer* ed. prefers Q

He breathed his last, and with his crown bequeathed 'ee
Your mother's wedding ring; which here I tender.
*Crotolon.* Most strange!
*Calantha.* Peace crown his ashes. We are queen then.
*Nearchus.* Long live Calantha, Sparta's sovereign queen!
*All.* Long live the queen!
*Calantha.* What whispered Bassanes?
*Bassanes.* That my Penthea, miserable soul,
Was starved to death.
*Calantha.* She's happy; she hath finished
A long and painful progress.—A third murmur
Pierced mine unwilling ears.
*Orgilus.* That Ithocles
Was murthered,—rather butchered, had not bravery
Of an undaunted spirit, conquering terror,
Proclaimed his last act triumph over ruin.
*Armostes.* How? murthered?
*Calantha.* By whose hand?
*Orgilus.* By mine. This weapon
Was instrument to my revenge. The reasons
Are just, and known; quit him of these, and then
Never lived gentleman of greater merit,
Hope, or abiliment to steer a kingdom.
*Crotolon.* Fie, Orgilus!
*Euphranea.* Fie, brother!
*Calantha.* You have done it.
*Bassanes.* How it was done let him report, the forfeit
Of whose allegiance to our laws doth covet
Rigour of justice; but that done it is,
Mine eyes have been an evidence of credit
Too sure to be convinced. Armostes, rend not
Thine arteries with hearing the bare circumstances
Of these calamities. Thou'st lost a nephew,
A niece, and I a wife: continue man still.
Make me the pattern of digesting evils,
Who can outlive my mighty ones, not shrinking
At such a pressure as would sink a soul
Into what's most of death, the worst of horrors.
But I have sealed a covenant with sadness,
And entered into bonds without condition,
To stand these tempests calmly. Mark me, nobles,

48 *abiliment* ability
54 *convinced* confuted
*rend* ed. rent Q
58 *digesting* stomaching, enduring

I do not shed a tear, not for Penthea.
Excellent misery!
*Calantha.* We begin our reign
With a first act of justice: thy confession,
Unhappy Orgilus, dooms thee a sentence;
But yet thy father's or thy sister's presence
Shall be excused. Give, Crotolon, a blessing
To thy lost son; Euphranea, take a farewell,
And both be gone.
*Crotolon.* Confirm thee, noble sorrow,
In worthy resolution.
*Euphranea.* Could my tears speak,
My griefs were slight.
*Orgilus.* All goodness dwell amongst ye.
Enjoy my sister, Prophilus; my vengeance
Aimed never at thy prejudice.
*Calantha.* Now withdraw.
*Exeunt* CROTOLON, PROPHILUS, & EUPHRANEA
Bloody relater of thy stains in blood,
For that thou hast reported him, whose fortunes
And life by thee are both at once snatched from him,
With honourable mention, make thy choice
Of what death likes thee best; there's all our bounty.—
But to excuse delays, let me, dear cousin,
Intreat you and these lords see execution
Instant, before 'ee part.
*Nearchus.* Your will commands us.
*Orgilus.* One suit, just queen, my last: vouchsafe your clemency,
That by no common hand I be divided
From this my humble frailty.
*Calantha.* To their wisdoms
Who are to be spectators of thine end
I make the reference. Those that are dead
Are dead; had they not now died, of necessity
They must have paid the debt they owed to nature
One time or other.—Use dispatch, my lords;
We'll suddenly prepare our coronation.
*Exeunt* CALANTHA, PHILEMA, CHRISTALLA.
*Armostes.* 'Tis strange these tragedies should never touch on
Her female pity.

74 *goodness* ed. gooddesse Q 76 *at thy prejudice* at injuring you
82 *excuse* obviate
93 *suddenly* immediately

*Bassanes.* She has a masculine spirit;
And wherefore should I pule, and, like a girl,
Put finger in the eye? Let's be all toughness,
Without distinction betwixt sex and sex.
*Nearchus.* Now, Orgilus, thy choice?
*Orgilus.* To bleed to death.
*Armostes.* The executioner?
*Orgilus.* Myself, no surgeon;
I am well skilled in letting blood. Bind fast
This arm, that so the pipes may from their conduits
Convey a full stream; here's a skilful instrument.
[*Shows his dagger*]
Only I am a beggar to some charity
To speed me in this execution
By lending th' other prick to th' tother arm,
When this is bubbling life out.
*Bassanes.* I am for 'ee;
It most concerns my art, my care, my credit.—
Quick, fillet both his arms.
*Orgilus.* Gramercy, friendship.
Such courtesies are real which flow cheerfully
Without an expectation of requital.
Reach me a staff in this hand. [*They give him a staff*]
If a proneness
Or custom in my nature, from my cradle,
Had been inclined to fierce and eager bloodshed,
A coward guilt, hid in a coward quaking,
Would have betrayed fame to ignoble flight
And vagabond pursuit of dreadful safety:
But look upon my steadiness, and scorn not
The sickness of my fortune, which, since Bassanes
Was husband to Penthea, had lain bed-rid.
We trifle time in words:—thus I show cunning
In opening of a vein too full, too lively.
*Armostes.* Desperate courage.
*Orgilus.* Honourable infamy.
*Lemophil.* I tremble at the sight.
*Groneas.* Would I were loose.
*Bassanes.* It sparkles like a lusty wine new broached;
The vessel must be sound from which it issues.
Grasp hard this other stick—I'll be as nimble—

109 *fillet* bind
*his* ed. this Q
117 *dreadful* full of fear
121 *cunning* skill, knowledge

But prithee, look not pale—have at 'ee! stretch out
Thine arm with vigour and unshook virtue.
[*Opens the vein*]
Good. Oh, I envy not a rival, fitted
To conquer in extremities. This pastime
Appears majestical; some high-tuned poem
Hereafter shall deliver to posterity
The writer's glory and his subject's triumph.
How is 't man? Droop not yet.
*Orgilus.* I feel no palsies.
On a pair-royal do I wait in death:
My sovereign, as his liegeman; on my mistress,
As a devoted servant; and on Ithocles,
As, if no brave, yet no unworthy enemy.
Nor did I use an engine to entrap
His life, out of a slavish fear to combat
Youth, strength, or cunning; but for that I durst not
Engage the goodness of a cause on fortune,
By which his name might have outfaced my vengeance.
Oh, Tecnicus, inspired with Phœbus' fire!
I call to mind thy augury, 'twas perfect:
'Revenge proves its own executioner'.
When feeble man is bending to his mother,
The dust 'a first was framed on, thus he totters.
*Bassanes.* Life's fountain is dried up.
*Orgilus.* So falls the standard
Of my prerogative in being a creature.
A mist hangs o'er mine eyes, the sun's bright splendour
Is clouded in an everlasting shadow.
Welcome, thou ice, that sittest about my heart;
No heat can ever thaw thee.
*Dies.*
*Nearchus.* Speech hath left him.
*Bassanes.* 'A has shook hands with time. His funeral urn
Shall be my charge. Remove the bloodless body.
The coronation must require attendance;
That past, my few days can be but one mourning.
*Exeunt.*

136 *pair-royal* in cards, three of the same denomination
142 *cunning* skill 143 *Engage* Stake
150 *standard* ed. Standards Q (see also p. 95)

## Act V, Scene iii

*An altar covered with white; two lights of virgin wax, during which music of recorders; enter four bearing* ITHOCLES *on a hearse, or in a chair, in a rich robe, and a crown on his head; place him on one side of the altar. After him enter* CALANTHA *in a white robe and crowned;* EUPHRANEA, PHILEMA, CHRISTALLA, *in white,* NEARCHUS, ARMOSTES, CROTOLON, PROPHILUS, AMELUS, BASSANES, LEMOPHIL, *and* GRONEAS. CALANTHA *goes and kneels before the altar, the rest stand off, the women kneeling behind. Cease recorders, during her devotions. Soft music.* CALANTHA *and the rest rise, doing obeisance to the altar.*

*Calantha.* Our orisons are heard; the gods are merciful.—
Now tell me, you whose loyalties pays tribute
To us your lawful sovereign, how unskilful
Your duties or obedience is to render
Subjection to the sceptre of a virgin,
Who have been ever fortunate in princes
Of masculine and stirring composition?
A woman has enough to govern wisely
Her own demeanours, passions, and divisions.
A nation warlike, and inured to practice
Of policy and labour, cannot brook
A feminate authority: we therefore
Command your counsel, how you may advise us
In choosing of a husband whose abilities
Can better guide this kingdom.
*Nearchus.* Royal lady,
Your law is in your will.
*Armostes.* We have seen tokens
Of constancy too lately to mistrust it.
*Crotolon.* Yet, if your highness settle on a choice
By your own judgement both allowed and liked of,
Sparta may grow in power, and proceed
To an increasing height.
*Calantha.* Hold you the same mind?
*Bassanes.* Alas, great mistress, reason is so clouded
With the thick darkness of my infinite woes,
That I forecast nor dangers, hopes, or safety.
Give me some corner of the world to wear out

3 *unskilful* unwise
9 *divisions* inner doubts
23 *infinite* ed. infinites Q

The remnant of the minutes I must number,
Where I may hear no sounds but sad complaints
Of virgins who have lost contracted partners;
Of husbands howling that their wives were ravished
By some untimely fate; of friends divided
By churlish opposition; or of fathers
Weeping upon their children's slaughtered carcases;
Or daughters groaning o'er their fathers' hearses:
And I can dwell there, and with these keep consort
As musical as theirs. What can you look for
From an old, foolish, peevish, doting man,
But craziness of age?
*Calantha*. Cousin of Argos,—
*Nearchus*. Madam?
*Calantha*. Were I presently
To choose you for my lord, I'll open freely
What articles I would propose to treat on
Before our marriage.
*Nearchus*. Name them, virtuous lady.
*Calantha*. I would presume you would retain the royalty
Of Sparta in her own bounds; then in Argos
Armostes might be viceroy; in Messene
Might Crotolon bear sway; and Bassanes—
*Bassanes*. I, queen? alas! what I?
*Calantha*. Be Sparta's marshal.
The multitude of high employments could not
But set a peace to private griefs. These gentlemen,
Groneas and Lemophil, with worthy pensions,
Should wait upon your person in your chamber.
I would bestow Christalla on Amelus,
She'll prove a constant wife; and Philema
Should into Vesta's temple.
*Bassanes*. This is a testament:
It sounds not like conditions on a marriage.
*Nearchus*. All this should be performed.
*Calantha*. Lastly, for Prophilus,
He should be, cousin, solemnly invested
In all those honours, titles, and preferments
Which his dear friend, and my neglected husband,
Too short a time enjoyed.
*Prophilus*. I am unworthy
To live in your remembrance.
*Euphranea*. Excellent lady.

34 *consort* harmony
47 (see p. 95)
52 (see p. 95)

*Nearchus*. Madam, what means that word 'neglected
husband'?
*Calantha*. Forgive me:—now I turn to thee, thou
shadow
Of my contracted lord. Bear witness all,
I put my mother's wedding-ring upon
His finger; 'twas my father's last bequest.
Thus I new-marry him whose wife I am;
Death shall not separate us. Oh, my lords,
I but deceived your eyes with antic gesture,
When one news straight came huddling on another
Of death, and death, and death. Still I danced forward;
But it struck home, and here, and in an instant.
Be such mere women, who with shrieks and outcries
Can vow a present end to all their sorrows,
Yet live to vow new pleasures, and outlive them.
They are the silent griefs which cut the heart-strings;
Let me die smiling.
*Nearchus*. 'Tis a truth too ominous.
*Calantha*. One kiss on these cold lips, my last. Crack,
crack!
Argos now's Sparta's king.—Command the voices
Which wait at th' altar now to sing the song
I fitted for my end.
*Nearchus*. Sirs, the song.

*A Song*

*All*. *Glories, pleasures, pomps, delights, and ease,*
*Can but please*
*Th' outward senses, when the mind*
*Is or untroubled, or by peace refined.*
1. [*Voice*] *Crowns may flourish and decay,*
*Beauties shine, but fade away.*
2. [*Voice*] *Youth may revel, yet it must*
*Lie down in a bed of dust.*
3. [*Voice*] *Earthly honours flow and waste,*
*Time alone doth change and last.*
*All*. *Sorrows mingled with contents, prepare*
*Rest for care;*
*Love only reigns in death; though art*
*Can find no comfort for a broken heart.*
[CALANTHA *dies*].

64 *mother's* ed. mother Q
68 *antic gesture* an acting performance
75 (see p. 95)
83 *Th'* ed. not in Q
84 *Is or* ed. Is not Q

*Armostes.* Look to the queen!
*Bassanes.* Her heart is broke indeed.
Oh, royal maid, would thou hadst missed this part!
Yet 'twas a brave one. I must weep to see
Her smile in death.
*Armostes.* Wise Tecnicus, thus said he:
*When youth is ripe, and age from time doth part,*
*The Lifeless Trunk shall wed the Broken Heart.*
'Tis here fulfilled.
*Nearchus.* I am your king.
*All.* Long live
Nearchus, king of Sparta!
*Nearchus.* Her last will
Shall never be digressed from: wait in order
Upon these faithful lovers, as becomes us.—
The counsels of the gods are never known,
Till men can call th' effects of them their own.
[*Exeunt*].

*FINIS*

The Epilogue

Where noble judgements and clear eyes are fixed
To grace endeavour, there sits truth, not mixed
With ignorance: those censures may command
Belief which talk not till they understand.
Let some say 'This was flat', some 'Here the scene
Fell from its height', another, that the mean
Was ill observed in such a growing passion
As it transcended either state or fashion.
Some few may cry ' 'Twas pretty well', or so,
'But'—and there shrug in silence; yet we know
Our writer's aim was in the whole addressed
Well to deserve of *all*, but please the *best*:
Which granted, by th' allowance of this strain,
The BROKEN HEART may be pieced up again.

THE END

3 *censures* opinions
6 *mean* artistic restraint

# CRITICAL NOTES

## *Epistle Dedicatory*

Page

3 *Lord Craven.* William, Lord Craven (1606–1697), was knighted in 1627. He commanded English troops fighting for Gustavus Adolphus in 1631, and was a firm Royalist during the English Civil War. He was deprived of his estates for loyalty to Charles I, and did not recover them until the Restoration. He was made an earl in 1664. From 1632 he was closely attached to Elizabeth of Bohemia, and it was said, without much probability, that he was privately married to her. He was made lieutenant-general of the forces in 1685, and was one of the early Fellows of the Royal Society.

## *The Scene*

5 *The speakers' names.* The name Amyclas probably derives from the town of Amyclae, an early settlement some three miles south of Sparta. It is mentioned in the Homeric *Catalogue* as in the domain of Menelaus. But Amyclas is also the name of the Laconian king in Sidney's *Arcadia*, and this is almost certainly Ford's source. In 1633 Quarto the name Lemophil is generally, though not invariably, printed as 'Hemophil'. I suspect that the real reading is 'Lenophil', meaning 'lover of the wine-vat', but there can be no certainty that this is what Ford intended, especially as he glosses it 'Glutton'. Groneas is a name whose origin I have been unable to trace. Amelus means 'neglectful', not 'trusty'.

## *The Prologue*

7 15–16. *What may be . . . a truth.* This may perhaps be a reference to the relationship between Sir Philip Sidney and his Stella, the Lady Rich. See S. P. Sherman, 'Stella and *The Broken Heart*', *PMLA*, XXIV (1909) 274–285.

10 I.i, 31. *In a firm growth of union.* Uncorrected copies of sheet B in Q read 'In a firme grouth of holy vnion' (see,

for example, British Museum, 644 b 35). The mistake is probably an echo from the previous line.

11 I.i, 94. *Worthy*. Q prints this word at the end of the preceding line.

12 I.i, 98. *By Vesta's sacred fires*. Vesta, the Roman hearth-goddess, was served by the Vestal Virgins, so that Euphranea's oath is aptly chaste. At the end of the play (V.iii, 53) Calantha ordains a chaste settlement for Philema, sending her into Vesta's Temple.

13 I.ii, 10–20. *It will . . . Pephon*. This speech of Amyclas is deliberately vague in its time-references. Laconia, or Lacedemonia, the south-eastern district of the Pelepon-nese, was the area ruled over by the city of Sparta. It was bordered on the west by Messenia, with its capital city Messene. There were constant disputes between the territories throughout the history of Greece.

14 I.ii, 66. *this provincial garland* 'i.e. the wreath (of laurel) which she had prepared; and which the ancients conferred on those who, like Ithocles, had added a *province* to the empire. These honorary chaplets, or crowns, were, as every schoolboy knows, composed of plants, leaves or flowers, according to the nature of the service rendered. Thus we have the *provincial*, the civic, the mural, the obsidional, and various other garlands, all woven of different materials, and all appropriate to their respective wearers, "deserv'd, not purchas'd."' Gifford.

15 I.ii, 92. *strengthed*. From the verb 'to strength' meaning 'to strengthen'. The form was obsolete by Ford's time. See O.E.D. Strength v.

16 I.ii, 105. *I need not a supporter*. I need no escort. In the formal procession to get the court off stage Euphranea is alone until Prophilus seizes the chance to accompany her. This is a crude hint, on Ford's part, of the relationship which appears in I.iii.

17 I.ii, 127. *By Vulcan*. Groneas swears by Mars, the soldier's god; Philema caps this with an oath by Vulcan, the husband of Venus, who caught her in the act of adultery with Mars.

17 I.ii, 132. *In forma pauperis*. 'Is where any Man, who hath just cause of Sute in *Chancery*, and will make *Affidavit*, that he is not worth Five pounds, his debts being paid, then upon a Petition to the Master of the *Rolls*, he shall be admitted to sue *In forma pauperis*, and shall have Council, and Clerks assigned him, without paying Fees, and the like by the Judges of other Courts.' Thomas Blount, *A Law-Dictionary*, 1670.

*page*

19 I.iii, 44. s.d. PROPHILUS *passeth over*. See Allardyce Nicoll, 'Passing Over the Stage', *Shakespeare Survey*, 12 (1959) 47–55, and cf. III.ii, 16 s.d.

21 I.iii, 102–23. *Say it . . . writers*. Orgilus, arguing with the book he is reading, strings together disjointed pieces of philosopher's jargon. His references are to the kind of problems discussed both by the Greek philosophers and the mediaeval schoolmen, and they would have sounded suitably old-fashioned to Ford's contemporary audience.

23 II.i, 1. *I'll have . . . dammed up*. Cf. Jonson, *Volpone*, II, v 'First, I will have this bawdy light dammed up'. The scene between Bassanes and Phulas is very similar to this scene in Jonson.

24 II.i, 41. *Now for the newest news*. Sherman points out that the following passage on news is probably modelled on *Volpone*, II,i. Phulas' news is all exaggerated gossip around a kernel of truth, until his report of the new law against jealous husbands, which is not mentioned elsewhere in the play.

25 II.i, 69. *Spangled with pearls*. Gifford suggested that Ford, a Devonshire man, would have pronounced 'pearls' as a disyllable, making this line metrically regular.

28 II.i, 147–8. *th'hadst . . . worshipp'st*. Some editors emend Q's 'sinnes' to 'saints'. The two forms could be confused in manuscript, but Q makes perfectly acceptable sense as it stands.

28 II.ii, 1–2. *Ambition . . . motion*. This idea of the birth of vipers was a common image for inhumanity. See Sir Thomas Browne, *Pseudodoxia Epidemica*, Bk. III, ch. 16.

32 II.ii, 104. *Argos*. A town and territory to the north-east of Laconia.

32 II.ii, 115–27. *Alone . . . fell*. Bassanes' soliloquy is a set-piece demonstration of the character of the morbidly jealous man. Sherman points out the close similarity between this description and that in Burton's *Anatomy of Melancholy*, Part III, sect. iii, mem. ii.

34 II.iii, 21. *school-terms*. Cf. II.ii, 100, where the terms of mediaeval philosophy fail to heal Ithocles' grief-stricken mind. Orgilus uses them here to create an 'antic disposition', a pose of incomprehensibility, through which his meaning gradually emerges. See also Ford's *'Tis Pity She's a Whore*, I.i, 1–4.

34 II.iii, 21–4. *What heaven . . . perfection*. The sense is 'Must not heaven, which forms man out of the earth, also sanctify pure beauty with the name of perfection?' It sounds nonsense to Penthea.

page

34 II.iii, 30–3. *As sweetly . . . fervour.* Q reads:

As sweetly scented as the Incense smoking
The holiest Artars, Virgin teares (like
On *Vesta's* odours) sprinkled dewes to feed 'em,
And to increase their feruour.

The emendation adopted in the present text was first proposed by Smeaton. The corruption may well have arisen from the compositor's misreading of a correction in his copy.

37 II.iii, 124. *frenzy.* Some editions, including Gifford-Dyce and Sherman, retain Q's 'French', which makes very difficult sense. The two forms 'frenzy' and 'French' could easily be confused in seventeenth century handwriting.

39 III.i, 10–11. *our. . . . hearts.* Most editors emend Q's 'hearts' to 'heart', but Tecnicus's statement is a generalization, not directed specifically at Orgilus whom he always addresses as 'thou'.

40 III.i, 70. *Delphos.* Ford seems to be combining Delphi, on the slopes of Parnassus, with the island of Delos, birthplace of Apollo and Artemis.

41 III.ii, 16. s.d. See note to I.iii, 44.

41 III.ii, 20–1. *Soldiers . . . effeminate.* Plutarch notes that the Spartans did not allow certain kinds of music to be played in the city, for fear it should enervate the citizens.

42 III.ii, 32. s.d. *discovered.* Probably by drawing aside a curtain at the back of the stage.

45 III.ii, 130–1. *Hath . . . sun.* The allusions are to Ixion, who embraced a cloud, thinking it to be Juno, and Phaeton, who drove his father Phoebus's chariot for one day. Both are examples of glory going before a fall. Cf. IV.i, 69–70.

46 III.ii, 149. An allusion 'to the small enclosures (*franks*, as distinguished from styes) in which boars were fattened' Gifford.

48 III.ii, 200. *Diseases . . . alike.* A common proverb. See Tilley, *Dictionary of the Proverbs in England in the 16th and 17th centuries*, D.357.

48 III.ii, 206. *To . . . jealousy.* Many emendations have been proposed. I have adopted Harrier's, and take the line to mean 'to transform my role into reality, and declaim against jealousy'. But the whole line may well be hopelessly corrupt.

51 III.iv, 5. *Borrow of nature justice.* Obtain justice by appeal to natural law, when it is not available by normal legal procedures.

*page*

56 III.v, 62. *Memory . . . Truth.* Proverbial: see Tilley, *op. cit.*, T. 580.

60 IV.i, 69. *Ixion.* Cf. III.ii, 130–131. Ithocles is likened to Ixion by Bassanes, in a frenzy, and by Armostes, in sober sense. The familiar myth (see Ovid, *Metamorphoses*, 12) is ironically employed here, since Ithocles is never guilty of overweening conduct. The causes of his eventual fate are important only to Orgilus.

60 IV.i, 88. Gifford inserted 'less' before 'rash' in this line, on the grounds that Q's reading 'is devoid of congruity and sense'. Most later editors have followed him. Although Q is rhythmically unsatisfactory I have retained it, since the whole of Nearchus' speech is sharply sarcastic and the line, as it stands, is properly tart.

61 IV.i, 102–4. *painted colts . . . lion.* 'It was a popular belief that lions were afraid of virgins, cocks, and the blood royal; a herald's coat adorned with the king's insignia might be presumed to have the same awe-inspiring power' (Sherman's edition, p. 274). The allusion in 'painted colts' remains obscure, though as Gifford points out 'Our old writers used colt . . . for a compound of rudeness and folly'.

61 IV.i, 120–1. *The hurts . . . deadly.* Q's reading 'The hurts are yet but mortal' has been defended, notably by Harrier who argues that 'mortal' is synonymous with 'deadly' in the next line, but that the emphasis is on the verb *prove* between them. I find this more ingenious than convincing, and have adopted the emendation 'not' for 'but'. The two forms might easily be confused by a compositor setting up from manuscript.

62 IV.i, 138. Tecnicus's prophecy has already begun to come true. Throughout this scene craft has been conferring with courtesy in Orgilus' treatment of Ithocles.

63 IV.ii, 14–15. *Thou art . . . Good-will.* The 'Garland of Good-will' was one of the popular miscellanies of the time. It is attributed to Thomas Deloney and contains poems by Raleigh, Breton and others. It seems to have been entered on the Stationers' Register on 5th March, 1593, and one edition appeared in 1631, two years before Ford's play. Weber notes another reference to it in Rowley's *Match at Midnight*, which was also printed in 1633. 'The Honeycomb of Honesty' is probably another such miscellany, but I can find no trace of it.

63 IV.ii, 18. *Beasts, only capable of sense.* A common Aristotelian concept: see *The Nicomachean Ethics*, i.13.

63 IV.ii, 24–5. *quintessence . . . elixir.* The quintessence was

the fifth element, beyond fire, air, earth and water, and was the object of the alchemist's search. The elixir was the alchemist's preparation designed to change base metals into gold.

66 IV.ii, 112. *Complain not*. In this speech Penthea's errant, disjointed phrases make sense to no one on stage except Orgilus. By facts, hints and allusions his method of revenge becomes clear. Only in the freedom given her by madness can she 'tutor' him.

66 IV.ii, 120. *When we last gathered roses*. i.e. II.iii, where Orgilus' last words are 'Action, not words, shall show me'.

67 IV.ii, 130. 'Amethyst', from Greek αμεθυστ-ος 'not drunken' was the name applied to the stone from the notion that it prevented intoxication. Penthea's allusion reminds Orgilus (the 'married bachelor') that the time has come for action in hot blood.

67 IV.ii, 140. *By yea and nay*. See *James*, 5, 12. This was the limit a Puritan allowed himself in the matter of swearing.

68 IV.ii, 162. *There is a mastery*. 'There is a contemporary ballad in the Shirburn collection "Of a maide now dwelling at the towne of *meurs* in *dutchland*, that hath not taken any foode this 16 yeares, and is not yet neither hungry nor thirsty; the which maide hath lately beene presented to the lady *elizabeth*, the king's daughter of *england*." This "maide" subsisted in the manner proposed by Bassanes—on perfumes'. (Sherman's edition, p. 275).

69 IV.ii, 200. *lord ascendant*. In astrology, the ascendant was the point of the ecliptic which at any moment (especially birth) was just rising above the eastern horizon. The 'lord of the ascendant' was any planet within the house of the ascendant. Nearchus sees that Calantha's love is governed and dominated by Ithocles.

70 IV.iii, 39. *Truth is the child of Time*. Cf. III.v, 62.

71 IV.iii, 69. *But wherefore sits*. Amyclas has spoken before about the preternatural gravity of the court: see III.iii, 36–9 and 58–63. Festivities are always *about to occur*, until V.ii.

72 IV.iii, 88. *Have I now kept my word?* There has obviously been a previous (offstage) avowal of love and agreement to marry between Calantha and Ithocles.

74 IV.iv, s.d. The 'engine' was a mechanical contrivance probably for trapping the arms of anyone who sat in the chair. The device has a long history: see the Gifford-Dyce edition, p. 302, where a list of previous examples appears. It was used by Ford's friend, Barnaby Barnes,

*page*

in *The Devil's Charter*, I.v, (ed. R. B. McKerrow in *Materialen zur Kunde d. älteren Engl. Dramas*, Louvain, 1907, vol. vi) where Lucretia says:

I have devised such a curious snare
As jealious Vulcan never yet devis'd
To graspe his armes unable to resist
Death instruments enclosed in these hands.

75 IV.iv, 26. *Phaeton.* The son of Helios, who was unable to control his father's chariot, and scorched the earth. Zeus struck him down with a thunderbolt.

76 IV.iv, 42. *Tent it with double force.* Cf. Webster, *The White Devil*, V.vi, 29–30:

Search my wound deeper: tent it with the steel
That made it.

77 V.i, 12. *doubles.* A double is a sharp turn, in running. Q's 'doublers' is not recorded with this meaning in O.E.D. The reference seems to be to the bad omen of a hare crossing one's path: cf. Jonson, *Tale of a Tub*, IV.ii, 18 'The unlucky Hare hath crost us all this day'.

78 V.i, 13. *splay-footed witch.* A splay foot was held to be one of the distinguishing marks of a witch: cf. Sidney, *Arcadia*, I.iii 'Only her face and her splayfoote have made her accused for a witch'.

78 V.i, 14. *Three drops.* '. . . if it bleeds one drop only it forebodes sickness, if three drops the omen is still worse'. Brewer, *Dictionary of Phrase and Fable.* s.v. Nose.

78 V.i, 43. *The virgin-bays.* Bay leaves were supposed to be an antidote against lightning because the bay was the tree of Apollo: cf. Webster, *The White Devil*, V.iv, 8–10:

Reach the bays,
I'll tie a garland here about his head;
'Twill keep my boy from lightning.

84 V.ii, 150. *So falls the standard.* Orgilus' death speech is very similar to Flamineo's: see Webster, *The White Devil*, V.iv.

86 V.iii, 47. *The multitude of high employments.* Burton advocates this course as one of the cures for Love-Melancholy: 'To be busy still, and as *Guianerius* enjoins, about matters of great moment, if it may be. . . . No better Physick than to be always occupied, seriously intent'. *Anatomy of Melancholy*, III.ii, v.i.

86 V.iii, 52. *Philema.* See note to I.i, 98.

87 V.iii, 75. *They are the silent.* Harrier notes that this is an English version of Seneca, *Hippolytus*, 607: 'Curea leves loquntur, ingentes stupent', and compares *The Revenger's Tragedy*, I.iv, 23.